# ORNAMENTAL TURNING

*Also by T. D. Walshaw*

The I.S.O. System of Units


*Other books by the same author*
*writing as 'Tubal Cain'*

Building the Beam Engine 'Mary'

Building the Overcrank Engine 'Georgina'

Building Simple Model Steam Engines

Building the 'Williamson' Engine

Drills, Taps and Dies

Hardening, Tempering and Heat Treatment

Milling Operations in the Lathe

Model Engineer's Handbook

Simple Workshop Devices

Soldering and Brazing

Spring Design and Manufacture

Workholding in the Lathe

Workshop Drawing

# ORNAMENTAL TURNING

## TD Walshaw

SPECIAL INTEREST MODEL BOOKS

**SPECIAL INTEREST MODEL BOOKS**
P.O. Box 327
Poole
Dorset
BH15 2RG
England
www.specialinterestmodelbooks.co.uk

First published by Argus Books 1990
This paperback edition 1994, reprinted 1996
Reprinted by Special Interest Model Books 2008

Illusrations acknowledged to *Holtz IV* are from Jacob Holtzapffel's *Hand or Simple Turning,* 1881. Those marked *Holtz V* are from his *The Practice of Ornamental or Complex Turning,* 1894, both forming part of the five-volume work, *Turning and Mechanical Manipulation.* Unacknowledged illustrations are by the author.

ISBN 978-185486-108-5

Typesetting by Photoprint, Torquay, Devon
Printed and bound in Great Britain by
Biddles Ltd. King's Lynn, Norfolk

# *CONTENTS*

# LIST OF ILLUSTRATIONS

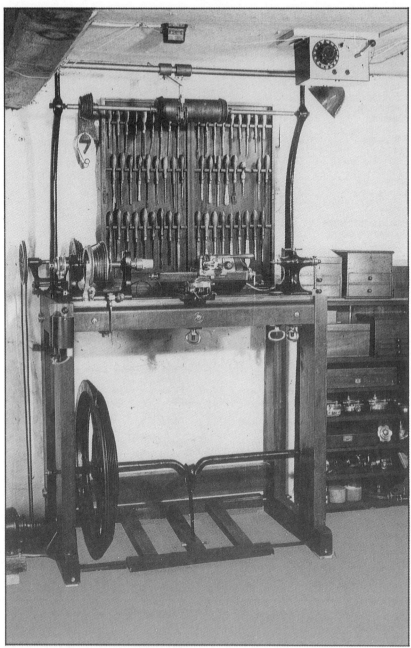

(Frontispiece) The author's Holtzapffel lathe No. 2456. A relatively modern machine, built about 1897.

# INTRODUCTION

We must first define what is meant by 'ornamental' turning for, after all, most turned work (in wood, at any rate) carries some degree of ornamentation. The name formerly given to the art was 'complex' turning, though some early writers used the term 'eccentric', before other forms of complexity became possible. But not all 'ornamental' work is complex, and only a small proportion is turned eccentrically. Further, when the art was revived just after the Second World War, it was felt that a 'Society of Complex Turners' (or even a 'Society of Eccentric Turners'!) might well lead to misunderstandings. So, today the distinction is made between 'plain' turning (which can be decorated) and 'ornamental' turning, which always includes some degree of complexity.

The fundamental distinction arises from the fact that plain turned pieces are always 'solids of revolution' but ornamental turned work is not. Fig. 1 shows a highly ornamented ceremonial pen. But it is 'plain turned', as the work was done between centres throughout. On the

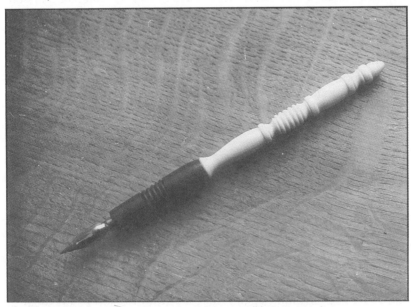

Fig. 1 A ceremonial pen, decorated. but 'plain turned' between centres.

Fig. 2 A tool handle, very plain, but cannot be turned between centres as one end is elliptical.

other hand, the very 'plain' tool handle in Fig. 2 could not possibly be turned between centres, as one end is oval and the other round. There is no decoration at all, but it was made in a lathe and is classed as ornamental turning. I should add that there is no suggestion that ornamental turning demands more skill than does plain turning. The two arts each make their own, quite different (and sometimes opposite) demands on the skills of the practitioner. They are simply quite different applications of the lathe.

The art of ornamental turning is older than many people imagine. The lathe was, of course, used from the very earliest times. Although illustrations of lathes in Europe do not appear until about the XVth or XVIth centuries, a few turned works have been discovered dating from the Iron Age. The craft developed over the centuries out of necessity – the manufacture of articles needed in everyday life. Later, the development of an aristocracy led to demand for articles 'beyond the common sort' so that the turner, like the potter and the metalsmith, was called upon to make greater efforts towards quality and, of course, decoration. This demand was at its highest around the Royal courts and the Church. On the continent of Europe, especially, one found the Court turner in residence alongside the Court musicians and artists.

Not unnaturally, these artist-craftsmen would vie with each other in providing their masters with works which excelled – the art of 'one-upmanship' is no new thing! A modification to the centrelathe to enable it to turn oval works came quite early, though this was developed as much for utility as for ornament. By about 1600 there is considerable evidence of ingenious turnery. The first book which I can find describing other than plain turning is one published by Jacques Besson, Engineer to Francis II, in 1569. This described both screwcutting machines and a lathe for 'oblique' turning. Salomon de Caus, well known for his 'Steam Pressure Ball', and who worked as Engineer to

Charles I, shows both a screwcutting lathe and an oval turning chuck in his book published in 1615. Father Cherubin, a Capuchin monk (many of the practitioners of those days were in Holy Orders) actually published a book on *How to make a Lathe* in 1671. By the end of that century much very complex turning was being done.

The first book dealing specifically with ornamental as well as 'plain' turning was published in 1701, by L'Abbe Plumier (recently translated by Dr. Paul Ferraglio, 102–20 Farragut Road, New York 11236). With no less than 71 large plates, he illustrates a variety of lathes, including 'rose engines'. Fig. 3 shows one of his machines, and Fig. 4 examples

Fig. 3 A French turner's workshop of about 1690. Note the overhead 'bow' used as a spring return for the treadle with a cord wrapped round the workpiece. (*From Plumier's 'L'Art de Tourner en Perfection', 1749*)

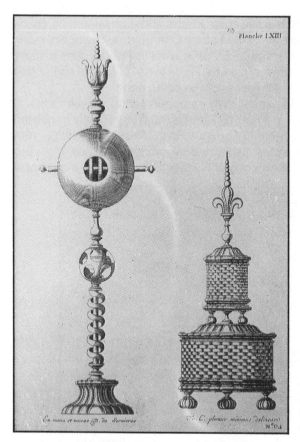

Fig. 4 Typical work done on machines such as Fig. 3 with added accessories. (*Plumier*)

of the type of artefact then in vogue! Other less comprehensive books continued to appear (including, in 1719, a sort of catalogue of turned ivories made by Conte de Serviere) but the classic is undoubtedly the *Manuel de Tourneur* by L.E. Bergeron, 1796. In two volumes, with 96 plates, it covers every aspect of turning. It was intended for the aristocracy rather than for the artisan (my own copy has the bookplate of Le Compte du Querhon) and shows clearly the state of the art at that time. Fig. 5 is a reproduction of Plate 12 Volume 2. The machine is very ornate, almost entirely made of wood, and is capable of screwcutting to six different pitches. There is a compound eccentric chuck, an oval (elliptical) turning chuck, swashplate apparatus, slide-rest, a spherical-turning attachment, and a rudimentary geometric chuck capable of producing epi-and hypo-cycloidal patterns. Quite a catalogue – and quite a price, too, no doubt! Fig. 6 shows the machine engaged in swashplate turning, with some of the products. 'Eccentric' turning in every sense of the word! This book was published in France

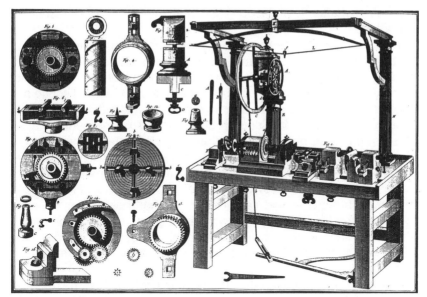

Fig. 5 A French ornamental turning lathe of about 1790. Accessories include an elliptical turning chuck, a simple geometric chuck, boring collar, swashplate attachment and a traversing mandrel to cut screw threads of up to six different pitches, as well as other work-chucks. (*From Bergeron's 'L'Art du Tourneur', 1796*)

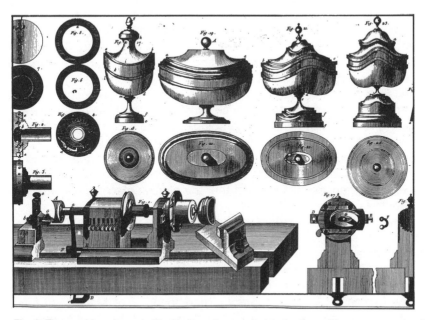

Fig. 6 The machine shown in Fig. 5 set up for swashplate turning, with some examples of work. (*Bergeron*)

just one year after John Jacob Holtzapffel (the first) sold his first lathe in England.

This is not the place for an account of the achievements of the Holtzapffel family, but the firm does merit some attention in any book on this subject. John Jacob the first (his grandson had the same names) came to this country from Alsace in about 1785 and set up his engineer's tool business at Long Acre in London about 1793. His first lathe was sold to a Mr. Crisp on June 31st 1795, the outfit costing £25–4s–10d. (This must have been quite an elaborate machine, as the simplest type cost about £5 at that time.) It had a plain headstock though the next. No.2 (all Holtzapffel lathes are numbered) had a traversing mandrel for screwcutting. We have few details of the earliest machines, but it is almost certain that they had beech or mahogany beds ('bearers') possibly with brass wearing surfaces near the head-stock. The first mention of one with a cast-iron bed was in 1798, No. 50; however, the headstocks, tailstocks and rests etc. were of cast iron.

The significance of John Jacob's work is twofold. First, he brought the cost of the machine down to a figure which a mere 'gentleman' (or even a prosperous tradesman) could afford. And, second, the design was both elegant and functional, unlike those of continental makers – if, indeed, there were any! (To put this period into an historic perspective, Holtz. No. 100 was being built at about the same time that Richard Trevethick was building his first locomotive engine.) To emphasise the contrast, Fig. 7 shows my own Holtzapffel lathe No. 484, built in 1805 and sold for 19 guineas to Geo. Reid Esq on March 3rd 1806. Comparison with Fig. 5 is illuminating, considering that less than 10 years separates the two. True, No. 484 lacks the traversing mandrel and the swashplate mechanism, but it is complete with eccentric, oval-turning and upright or dome chuck, all of brass, and has the overhead gear and the drilling and milling spindle. It was earning its keep as a plain lathe in a cabinet maker's workshop when I bought it and I still use it, especially for elliptical work, despite the fact that it has a mahogany bed. (By that time all-iron beds supported on beech frames were common, despite the fact that the planing machine was not yet invented.)

By the time that John Jacob I died in 1835, nearly 1600 machines had been sold. Not all were 'ornamental' lathes. The firm supplied the East India Company with machines for shipboard repair work, the Royal Ordnance Factory, and many commercial firms as well, but the spur given to ornamental turning as a leisure occupation in this country was immense. A contemporary – and friend – of Maudslay, John Jacob could well have pursued a path which led to pre-eminence in the industrial field but when his son, the 'Great' Charles Holtzapffel, took over the firm, Holtzapffel's were so well established in their niche that there must have been little need to depart from it.

Apart from supplying very high quality machines, the main contribution made by the firm was the introduction of rotary cutting devices which could be engaged with the work while the mandrel was stationary. Plain and profiled 'drills' had been used for a century or so, but the 'cutting frame' was a considerable advance. These will be considered in detail later, but they enabled very complex patterns to be cut. While many of these could be made using the eccentric chuck, this involved stopping the whole machine while the index on the *chuck* was adjusted, whereas the cutting frame could be kept running while the *mandrel* was indexed. This revolutionised the art; whereas the 18th century continental practitioners pursued elaboration and novelty of *form*, the English amateur tended towards relatively classical shapes ornamented with applied decoration.

It was Charles who embarked on the monumental task of writing the series of books on *Turning and Mechanical Manipulation*, Volume 1

Fig. 7 The author's Holtzapffel No. 484, built in 1805. The original ornamental chucks are still with the machine and, despite its age, it is capable of quite advanced work.

being published in 1843, and the third after his death in 1847. His son, John Jacob II continued the work, Volume V appearing in 1884; a total of over 3000 pages (all written with pen and ink at that!) and 1600-odd illustrations. This was, no doubt, an attempt to assist the many practitioners of the hobby who were the firm's customers – the two thousandth lathe was sold a few years later.

By now the art was more highly developed in this country than anywhere else, and a number of other manufacturers of ornamental lathes had appeared. It may be surprising to us today, but was commonplace at that time, that some of these actually sent men to work for Holtzapffel to 'learn the business', and some adopted Holtzapffel standards in their own works. (In passing, it is worth noting that John Jacob I standardised his screw threads in 1799, long before Whitworth was born, and continued their use until the business closed.) Of these other makers, all but a few were already engaged in one form of allied trade or another. Evans, with an output almost as large as Holtzapffel's, is described as 'Axle-maker to Her Majesty the Queen'. Daniel and Joseph Fenn (see Fig. 8) had many generations behind them as horological instrument makers. Birch was a well-

Fig. 8 An ornamental lathe made by Joseph Fenn, dated around 1850.

known Manchester maker of fine engineer's machine tools. George Hines was a general engineer and, of course, the Britannia company had been making lathes for a very long time. In addition there was a number of other makers who produced a few lathes and nothing else, of whom Goyen is perhaps the most well known – and the most sought after!

The manufacture of lathes specifically for ornamental turning ceased at the outbreak of the First World War. (Holtz. No. 2557, the last they made, was *sold* in November 1928 but was actually made in 1913/14.) Although a very large number of these lathes were around, the art virtually died with that war. A new leisure occupation, that of 'model engineering', had developed to engage the attention of those who found pleasure in the 'Art and Mysterie' of turning. It is true that both *English Mechanics* and *The Model Engineer* still included articles on ornamental turning from time to time but these were rare. Wood and ivory were out, metal-turning was in, and that seemed to be that.

However, in 1948, the late Mr. Fred Howe gathered together a few like-minded individuals to form a 'Society of Ornamental Turners'. Mr. Howe was an incredibly gifted craftsman, working in every conceivable medium (not only in turning, either) but his enthusiasm for ornamental turning was undoubtedly responsible for the upsurge of interest in recent years. The specialist lathes are not too easy to come by; they need not be very expensive, but no-one who owns one will willingly part with it so long as he or she can still use it! However, it is, as I shall show later, quite practicable to use an ordinary engineer's screwcutting lathe to carry out a wide range of work, with no special accessories other than those normally found in a reasonably equipped workshop. The making of the special cutting frames is a simple matter and enough home-made eccentric and other chucks have been made to 'show the way'. I myself quite happily switch from the Holtzapffels to my Myford or even my Lorch instrument lathe, as some of the later examples will show. Most of the illustrations in this book come from one or other, though some were made on a Fenn (my first O.T. lathe, Fig. 8) or on a Birch. *There is no reason at all why anyone owning a lathe with a sliderest cannot practise the art.*

There is, of course, no more effective occupation than 'turning' for inducing peace of mind and relaxation – it is a truism that 'turners live long and die happy'! Indeed, more than one ornamental turner has continued treadling well into his '90s. There is an added attraction, too. Compared with model-making – of any type – which is largely concerned with 'copying' something to a smaller scale, there is immense scope for the art of design in ornamental turning. Mere technical expertise will not do, as the 19th century extravaganza shown in Fig. 9 will amply demonstrate. That the maker was an outstanding turner (it was made wholly on a lathe) is undeniable, but I would hate to have it on my mantelpiece. The dimension of 'creative design' is an imperative in all worthwhile ornamental turning. Fortunately, it is also an extremely enjoyable part. To be able to start with a clean sheet of paper and end by lighting the candle in the finished product and then to be able to say 'It is all my own work' should be enough for anyone. (You can make your own candle, too, but that needs another book!)

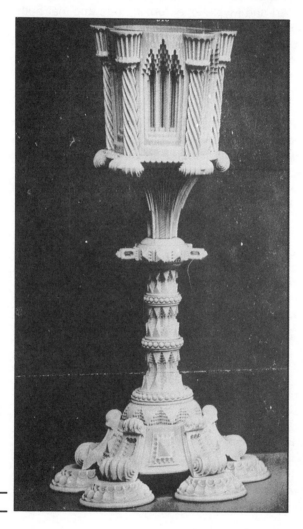

Fig. 9 A nineteenth-century ornamentally-turned chalice in ivory; all the work was done on a lathe – a triumph of technique over aesthetics? (*Holtz V*)

# 1 ORNAMENTAL LATHES AND THEIR EQUIPMENT

There are no 'modern' ornamental lathes, although I understand that a limited edition of five machines is currently being made in America, and there *may* have been one or two made to special order in this country after the Great War. But most machines are likely to be at least 80 years old and the majority are older still. The oldest known are, unfortunately, no more than museum pieces, and I believe that the oldest machine to be regularly used is my Holtzapffel No. 484 (Fig. 7) which is, at the time of writing, 184 years old. This is not to say that a modern engineer's lathe cannot be used; much good work is done on such, and we shall look at this in a later chapter.

So, what are the fundamental requirements for ornamental work? First, there must be some provision for indexing the headstock mandrel, preferably directly (i.e. without the use of worm gearing) as shown in Fig. 10. As an alternative there must be means of mounting a direct dividing engine on the sliderest. Next, a sliderest is almost

Fig. 10 The division circles on the pulley of the Fenn lathe.

essential. A little work can be done without one, but not much. Thirdly, there must be means either of rotating the work eccentrically to the lathe axis, or of carrying a rotating cutter eccentrically on the sliderest. These are the basics. Much of the elaboration found on ornamental machines is devised to facilitate or extend these provisions, or to add precision to the settings. In this connection it is worth emphasising that, although most work is done in wood or ivory, precision is really important. The eye is a very precise measuring instrument, and an error of a thousandth of an inch can result in an otherwise pleasing design becoming offensive.

Although, as we have already defined it, ornamental works are not 'solids of revolution' nevertheless the basis of most of the work remains a circle. Excluding elliptical work – and the patterns produced by such rarities as the cycloidal cutting frame or geometric chucks – most shapes and surface patterns are built up from circular incisions, the art being to arrange these in a visually attractive pattern, or, in the case of the true artist, to effect some degree of surprise by *leaving out* some part of the geometric symmetry. Many examples of these circle-based designs will be found in later pages, but Fig. 80 (p. 95) may serve to make the point.

Almost all the tools used to cut the patterns have a 'profile'; usually triangular but they can be square ended, radiused or formed into one of the classic shapes such as the ogee. The reflections from the flanks of these incisions transform the 'rude geometry' into a delight to the eye, just as the facets on a gem transform a mere stone to a thing of beauty. So, let us look at the machine, examine the major components and then the accessories.

## THE BED

The ornamental lathe is not a 'sliding' lathe. That is to say the saddle does not traverse the bed when cutting as does that of the normal engineer's lathe. The sliderest can, of course, be set at any point on the bed but it is then clamped in position and all sliding movements done with this. So, the fact that many old machines have wooden 'bearers' (the original name for the bed) is no serious disadvantage. Clearly, the timber used must be stable (usually mahogany or beech) and there is usually a brass insert to resist wear in the region nearest the headstock. However, following the invention of the planing machine in about 1817, the use of 'iron bearers' became the norm rather than an expensive handchipped and scraped luxury.

Three normal configurations may be found. Firstly, the cast iron bed on cast iron standards, Fig. 11 (and Fig. 8) being typical. Secondly, iron bearers supported on a timber framework having two pillars to which it was attached – Figs. 7 and 12. This is typical of all early machines, but the construction was used for a very long time, as it was cheaper than the third type – Fig. 13 – where the bearers are supported on a double set of uprights. In the better class of machine there was always a wooden 'frontpiece' hiding the cast iron bed, and all types were fitted with backboards on which to keep tools etc. The timber would normally be beech but mahogany was preferred by those

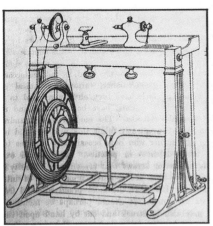

Fig. 11 (Above left) The typical nineteenth-century cast iron stand. See also Fig. 8. (*Holtz IV*)

Fig. 12 (Above right) A machine supported on single beech or mahogany uprights. Note the equipment chest or 'coffin' on the backboard, and compare with Fig. 7. (*Holtz IV*)

Fig. 13 (Right) A lathe with twin uprights supporting the bed. (*Holtz IV*)

who could afford the extra cost. The treadle and flywheel was supported between the uprights and the variety of designs here was legion! Some were very elaborate indeed. Unfortunately many machines have lost their treadles over the years, succumbing first to the gas engine and later to the electric motor.

The bed proper is a single casting with a machined top and a longitudinal machined slot which acts as a guide to the headstock, tailstock and sliderest support to ensure consistency of alignment – Fig. 14 (those with all-timber bearers needed setting up every time anything was moved). The timber parts are jointed with tongues and mortices, and held together with through bolts engaging concealed nuts within the timber. In looking at these machines it must be remembered that those owned by the nobility and gentry (and these included the Czar of Russia and the Crown Prince of Austria – the latter's machine being a present from Queen Victoria) were often objects of display. Indeed, the advantage of the timber frame against the iron standards was quoted in one catalogue as '. . . reducing noise and vibration, and not out of place in any library'! The workmanship was always superb. Even today the tenons should dismantle with no more than a tap with a mallet, and on the machine seen in Fig. 7 a push on one drawer will bring out the one below, due to air trapped behind.

Fig. 14 The bed of the Fenn lathe seen in Fig. 8, after restoration.

Fig. 15 A 'common mandrel' headstock (Fenn) fitted with the 'sector apparatus' referred to later.

## HEADSTOCK

There are two basic types, each of which may be furnished with varying degrees of elaboration. Fig. 15 is the 'common mandrel'. The spindle, either wrought iron or steel case-hardened ('steeled' to use the contemporary term; until about 1860 the term 'steel' always referred to high-carbon tool-steel as we understand it today) on the wearing surfaces, has a cone bearing at the front and a screw-centre at the rear. Adjustment of the latter takes up any wear. The second type, known both as the 'traversing mandrel' or 'screw mandrel', has parallel bearings at front and rear and is restrained endways by a collar at the front and an adjustable thrust washer and bolt at the rear. That shown in Fig. 16 is fitted with a threaded 'bobbin' or hob replacing the thrust washer. This engages with a turret of mating guide threads below. This is the screwcutting gear, and it will be understood that as the mandrel rotates it also slides sideways under the influence of the threads. We shall deal with this in detail later.

The 'screw mandrel' is considered to be the more desirable, but it is obvious that there can be no provision for taking up wear. The bearing surfaces are, of course, dead hard, as are the bushes in which they run. With the common mandrel, wear can easily be allowed for, though it is likely to be very small except on the back centre. After

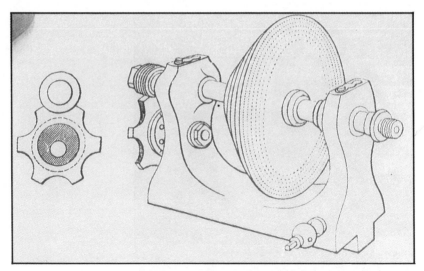

Fig. 16 Traversing mandrel headstock, fitted with screwcutting guide hobs. (*Holtz V*)

180-odd years, the front cone of the Holtzapffel No. 484 showed less than 0.001 inch wear! The common mandrel can, of course, be fitted with the 'spiral apparatus' or geared screwcutting equipment, mounted on the front of the headstock.

Whichever type of headstock, there will be dividing circles on the pulley. The least number likely to be found is three, having 96, 120 and 144 holes (though a few have 180 in place of 144) but up to six is usual – 96, 112, 120, 144, 192 and 360 holes. (Note the preoccupation with factors of three, although the 112 circle factors seven.) These circles are engaged with an index point attached to the lathe bed, which may be of a very simple type. But most have an adjustment at the lower end (often calibrated) so that the exact position of the mandrel may be set beforehand. A more elaborate index still is the 'counting index' which considerably reduces the risk of using the wrong hole. And, finally, a complex geared index unit which enables the user to space equal linear divisions round the periphery of an ellipse of any length/width ratio. So, even a simple accessory like this can display considerable degrees of sophistication, and this is not unusual!

### Headstock Accessories

Fig. 17 is a drawing of the headstock carrying most of the accessories likely to be found, with a photograph, Fig. 18, of my own, very similar one. Let me say at once that the absence of some of these features need not imply an inferior machine. I did some of my best work on my Fenn lathe, the headstock of which is seen in Fig. 15.

'A' is the cast-iron body, located to the bed by a tongue in the slot of the bed, and secured by a single bolt below. 'B' is the sliding mandrel, located endways by the collar 'F'. In the photograph this has been replaced by the screw guide bobbin, engaging with the turret 'E' below it. This turret is mounted on an eccentric bush, so that it can be

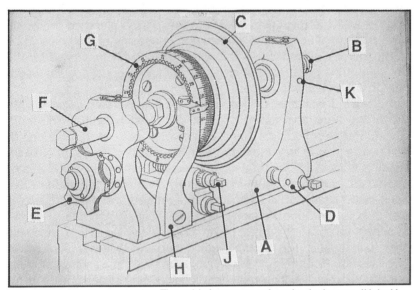

Fig. 17 Headstock accessories. The guide letters are referred to in the text. (*Holtz V*)

Fig. 18 Photograph of a headstock similar to Fig. 17. Note the adjustment screw on the dividing index.

meshed properly with the bobbin, or be disengaged. 'C' is the cone pulley, which has the division circles on the front, and the dividing index is carried in the boss 'D'. (Note the adjustable type of index in Fig. 18.) 'E' is the master turret for screw threads, shown engaged with the screw bobbin in the photograph. At 'G' is what is known as the 'sector apparatus'. A circle of holes can accept taper pegs. These will engage with the micrometer screw stops on the standard 'H' which have a range of adjustment exceeding the spacing of the holes. Thus the mandrel can be rotated through a defined angle, limited by the position of the pegs, so that incisions of exactly equal angular length can be cut on the workpiece.

Associated with this device is the 'tangent screw', comprising a worm, the head of which is seen at 'J', engaging with a 180 tooth wheel. The worm spindle has a micrometer index of 12 divisions. It can be used (a) to lock the mandrel in any position, (b) as an auxiliary dividing engine, (c) for rotating the mandrel when using the sector apparatus, or (d) as a 'slow motion drive'. (Very few O.T. lathes have back gear.) Lastly, at 'K' can be seen a small circle. This is one of a pair of holes on opposite sides, accurately set at lathe centre height, to accept the locating screws of the 'elliptical turning chuck' which we shall look at later. The centre height is usually five inches, but seven inches is not uncommon. A few lathes were made to a smaller capacity but the very size of the ornamental chucks almost demands a minimum of five inches. I have used this fairly elaborate headstock as an illustration as it carries almost every likely accessory. However, that on my Fenn machine (Fig. 15) was very much simpler, and was found quite adequate for a wide range of work.

## THE SLIDEREST

There have been many different forms of sliderest over the years, and it is very difficult to provide a 'typical' description. However, all have common features. First, the toolholder (usually called the tool 'receptacle') is always in the form of a trough, into which the shanks of the larger tools (always accurately machined) fit exactly, as do the shanks of the cutting frames. Smaller tools are held within a brass liner. All are held in place by two screws and bridge-pieces. Once the sliderest has been adjusted for centre height, all tools will have the points exactly at this height, as will the cutting frames unless wear has taken its toll. Tool-changing becomes a real joy, and makes the modern 'quick change' toolpost look very clumsy! Naturally, the tools must be appropriate to the machine. Holtzapffel and most makers used shanks which were 9/16 inch square, but those by Hines are 5/8 inch and Birch are really solid, being one inch square.

The second important feature is that cut is put on by *hand lever*, under the restraint of a feedscrew which really acts as a depth stop. There are, in fact, two of these; one for controlling the rate of infeed, the other as a calibrated depth-of-cut limiter. Facilities for the normal screw feed *may* be found on a few sliderests, but they are seldom needed. The lever feed is far superior for this class of work. The third feature is a consequence of the fact that the machine is not a 'sliding' lathe. The mainslide is very long compared with those found on the saddles of screwcutting lathes; 10 to 12 inches is normal, but rests with travels of up to 18 inches have been known. (On some very early machines, though, travel is usually limited to about six inches.)

Fig. 19 is a drawing of a typical 'ordinary' sliderest – at least, it demonstrates the main features. The cradle 'A' has a dovetail groove on the underside to engage with the holding-down bolt which passes through the slot in the bed. (All the rests and other accessories have identical grooves, so that changes can be made rapidly.) 'B' is the mainslide and its leadscrew (covered by a guard on all later Holtzapffel machines) is operated by a winch handle at the end. This has a micrometer dial reading to 0.001 inch. The slide is carried on a large diameter peg which fits a socket in the cradle, with a ring 'C' having tommy-bar holes at the upper end. This is really a threaded nut, and is used to adjust the height of the slide above the bed. 'D' is the topslide which carries the tool 'receptacle' 'E' in vee slides at right angles to the mainslide. Note the two screws 'H' which secure the tool, or its holder, in the trough; that at the rear has an extended body, on

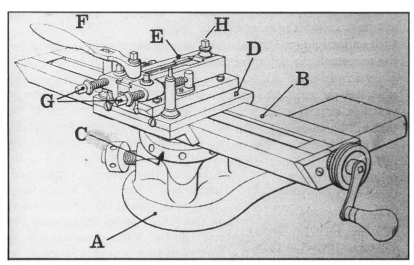

Fig. 19 The common sliderest. (*Holtz V*)

which the operating lever 'F' is set, pivoting on an upright column. This lever can be used on either side of the toolholder. At 'G' are the two depth screws already mentioned, that on the right being used to control the forward motion, the other being the calibrated depth stop. Both can be locked if need be. The sliderest can be swung round at any angle after slackening the boss-headed screw seen at the left of the cradle socket. Fig. 20 shows a photograph of my own sliderest, which has a few accessories which we will now consider.

Fig. 20 Sliderest of Holtzapffel No. 2456. Note the horn handle!

### Sliderest Refinements (Fig. 21)

At 'E' is seen one of two *adjustable stops*, which engage with a peg below the mainslide. Once set these enable the slide to be set exactly in line with, or at right angles to, the bed. Just discernible in the photo (Fig. 20) is a calibrated protractor scale for use at intermediate settings. At 'D' are the *Fluting Stops*. These are clamped to the bed of the mainslide and limit the travel of the toolslide. These can also be discerned in the photograph, Fig. 20. Now look at the base of the cradle or banjo in Figs. 20 and 21 and compare with Fig. 19. You will notice that the sides of the cradle in this case have been machined. These machined sides fit into a secondary cradle which is registered to the slot in the bed. Whereas the simple slide in Fig. 19 may swing about when moved along the bed, that shown in Fig. 20 will maintain its attitude throughout; any angular setting of the mainslide will be retained. This is known as the *registering cradle*, and is much to be desired, to the extent that those whose machines haven't one often

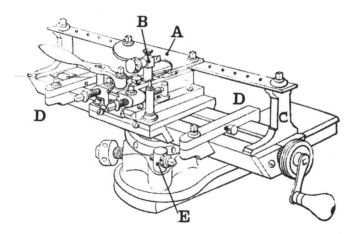

Fig. 21 A 'registering' sliderest, having a guide to maintain alignment with the bed. (*Holtz V*)

make up a cradle and have the 'banjo' machined to suit. I have marked this at 'X' in the photograph.

The *copying attachment* (usually known as the 'curvelinear attachment') comprises templates 'A' of any shape you please attached to a stiff bar carried at the ends of the mainslide on the pillars 'C'. At 'B' is the *follower* or rubber, which replaces the forward tool-retaining screw. Quite complex in construction, this follower is adjustable and is used to put on cut in place of the normal depthing screw. Thus the tool is constrained to follow the shape of the template. Templates are made of carbon steel, but for 'one-off' shapes almost any material can be used. The device can, of course, be used across the bed if desired, to form, for example, the shape of shallow bowls. As we shall see later, its use does demand some care and forethought (See Fig. 96b, p. 121.)

Less common still is the *mainscrew ratchet*, which is fitted instead of the micrometer index. This enables repeated successive movement of the toolslide to be made in precise and equal amounts. Also rare is the *automatic feed attachment*. This, driven by a belt or cord from the lathe 'overhead drive' provides the conventional automatic tool traverse found on ordinary metal-cutting lathes. Its absence need cause no concern, as long, slow traverses are very rare indeed in ornamental work.

The *sliderest tools* are dealt with in Chapter 3. Suffice to say at this stage that most are of high-carbon steel, beautifully heat-treated. Some practitioners now use high-speed steel, mainly due to the availability of this material as ground toolbits. A few – very few – diamond tipped O.T. tools have emerged over the years, but they are extremely rare!

Fig. 22 An early form of tailstock, 1805. The point of the wrought iron screw is hardened.

## TAILSTOCK

Early tailstocks comprised no more than a simple casting carrying a pointed, case-hardened, wrought iron screw (Fig. 22.) The locking screw carries a brass insert to avoid damaging the thread. Surprisingly, the alignment is usually quite accurate provided that the point has not been damaged. There is often a *female* centre in the boss-head of the screw for use on workpieces with pointed ends.

Fig. 23 shows the later type, although, again, there are many variations. The barrel or 'poppet' works in a bored hole, and carries the hard centre either on a taper or, as in the photograph, screwed into the end. The tailstock is seldom needed for drilling – flat drills carried on the sliderest being preferred, as modern twist drills tend to bind in the exotic woods and ivory. No provision is made for 'setover' as the long sliderest provides all that is needed for taper turning.

Fig. 23 The Fenn tailstock, typical of most machines after about 1820.

Fig. 24 A boring collar. The conventional type of 'steady' cannot be used on wood.

## THE BORING COLLAR

This is shown in Fig. 24. It comprises a thick disc mounted on a pedestal to fit the lathe bed, the disc having from six to ten holes of various sizes, tapered at about 90 degrees included angle within the thickness of the disc. It is used as a steady, to support the end of cylindrical workpieces while boring. It is only needed when boring longer pieces – say, over two diameters long. Care must be taken if the collar is obtained separate from the lathe, as there may be slight differences in centre height, which may cause the work to flex within the chuck and lose grip.

## WORKHOLDING

Most ornamental turners today make use of the standard three- and four-jaw chucks, though the latter are usually the very light four-inch pattern. However, the range of workholding devices is very large indeed. The duties range from secure hold, for roughing down from the square or log, to extreme precision for cases where the workpiece must be removed and reset very accurately.

The *wood block chuck*, generally made of boxwood (or lignum vitae), is a 'must'. This can be turned to form spigots, recesses, screw threads or shaped cavities to hold the work. As they are machined to suit each job as it comes they must be regarded as 'consumable' and the wise turner ensures that he has a number available. In some cases the work may be glued to the block, with a slip of paper between ('Seccotine' let down with water serves well) or it may be attached using double-sided tape.

The *faceplate*, usually of brass, is an imperative. As well as the conventional fixing with woodscrews from the back, work can, again, be glued to it. If no faceplate is available then one of wood makes an admirable (some say preferable) substitute. Fig. 25 shows one of mine, made of lignum vitae, with a brass insert to fit the mandrel nose thread.

The *wood spring chuck*, Fig. 26, is another very common type. The photo shows two home-made ones of boxwood, together with a very early one of beech. The walls are tapered on the outside and carry eight or more slits, so that when the ring is pressed on, the 'jaws' close on the work. The cavity can be bored to suit the job – usually with a step to provide lateral location, so that these, also, need replacement in time.

The *plain cup chuck* is usually made of brass, the cup bored slightly taper. The rough workpiece is simply knocked in with a mallet. It can, of course, be machined to suit the job but its main use is in roughing out. Naturally, it was developed into the *brass spring chuck* similar to the wooden ones. It has the advantage that it does not 'move' with changes in humidity. I prefer the wooden chucks, as there is less risk of tool damage during close working. Both wood and brass cup chucks (unsplit) are used as *wax chucks*. These carry the work in the cavity, where it is secured by pouring in bees- or candle-wax.

Fig. 25 Faceplate made from lignum vitae, with a brass insert to fit the mandrel nose. Double-sided tape has been used to hold the work.

Fig. 26 Wood spring chucks. Small ones made by the author; the larger is about 125 years old.

The so-called '*die chuck*' (see Fig. 53, p. 53) is basically similar to the two-jaw drill-chuck, for holding small diameters. A more advanced type has the dies (jaws) held in a spherical seating so that the work may be held at up to about 30 degrees from the lathe axis. Some machines may be provided with a very large '*Universal*' chuck – really a two-jaw chuck of up to nine inches diameter – the forerunner to the modern scroll chuck. Fig. 27 shows a home-made one, fitted to a Myford lathe, by Mr. J.A. Batchelor.

This brief account can touch only the borders of the workholding devices used. The plain screw (called a 'pig's tail'), the wood prong, the eight-screw cup chuck and many others devised by users in the past for specific jobs will be found in most lathe tool-chests (Fig. 27a).

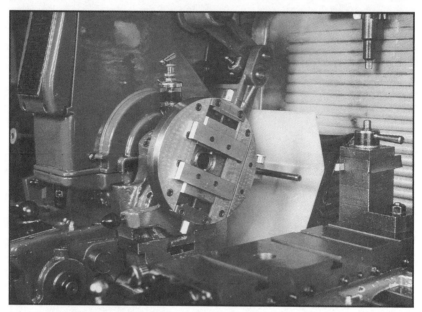

Fig. 27 A two-jaw chuck is often used to hold large pieces. This one was made by Mr. J.A. Batchelor, to fit his model engineer's lathe. (*Photo: J.A. Batchelor*)

## THE 'ORNAMENTAL' CHUCKS

These formed the basis of all ornamental turning in early days and, although most work today is done using the rotary cutting frames, it is right and proper to deal with them first, not least because the possession of but one of these chucks will enable considerable work to be done using ordinary tools. First, however, a *word of warning*. Although most makers – Evans and Birch in particular – used quite advanced production methods in the later years, almost all chucks were *finished* on the headstock of the lathe for which they were intended. If such a chuck was ordered later, the customer was asked to return the headstock to the maker's works for final fitting. This means that few ornamental chucks will work really satisfactorily if set

Fig. 27(a) A collection of chucks and other accessories, including a circular saw and arbor for use on the lathe. (*Fenn*)

up on another lathe. All Holtzapffel lathes were numbered, and these were stamped on all headstock fittings, but not all makers did this.

The chucks rely on the fit on the thread. There is no 'register' as on modern lathes. (Birch lathes are an exception.) So that, as well as a fundamental misfit, the user may meet trouble due to wear and damage as well. Now, this is not to say that a chuck cannot be made to fit. Many have been so treated, but it does need very careful and reasonably skilled work to do so. It is most regrettable that so many machines in the past have been sold at auction, with the result that some basic accessories have been parted from their parent machine.

### The Eccentric Chuck

This is shown in Figs. 28 and 29. In the engraving, the screw 'a' is an exact replica of the mandrel nose, on which can be mounted any workholding chuck. This threaded boss is part of a worm dividing wheel 'b' of 96 teeth which can be indexed either a tooth at a time or finer using the worm shaft 'c' and camlock 'd'. (Some earlier chucks have a serrated disc and ratchet which serves the same purpose.) This rotates on the slide 'e' which is carried in vee guides on the backplate 'f'. The slide is moved by a leadscrew and knob 'g', which is usually calibrated in 0.01 inch divisions. A taper pin is provided to lock the slide in the zero position, when 'a' will rotate coaxially with the

Fig. 28 The eccentric chuck. Guide letters are referred to in the text. (*Holtz V*)

Fig. 29 The author's eccentric chuck.

mandrel. It is obvious that, as soon as the slide is moved, the work will rotate eccentrically to the lathe centres.

The use of the chuck is detailed later, but it can be seen that, if the slide is offset and a pointed tool applied to the workpiece, a circular incision will be cut. If now the forepart is indexed, say eight teeth on the work, and the tool again applied, a further circle will be cut – and so on; finally producing a rudimentary pattern of 12 interlaced circles. Such a procedure can be elaborated so that very complex designs indeed can be executed. A glance at Fig. 30 will, I hope, convince you! The chuck has many other applications, demonstrated in Fig. 99a on page 126.

Fig. 30 Decoration such as this is well within the capacity of the eccentric chuck. Ivory, 2½ inches diameter.

### *The Oval or Elliptical Turning Chuck*

Referring to the engraving, Fig. 31, the first impression is that of an eccentric chuck. In fact, the forepart, 'a' to 'h' is identical. ('h' is the taper pin.) However, instead of being controlled by a feedscrew, the slide has two hard steel strips (barely visible in Fig. 31, but seen in the rear view of Fig. 32) at 'jj' attached to the back of the slide and passing through slots in the backplate. These bear on the circular brass cam-ring 'k'. If this ring is coaxial with the mandrel then, when the chuck

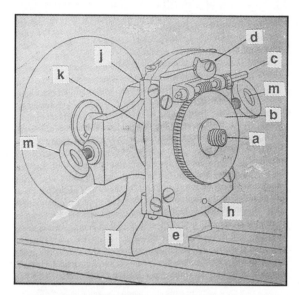

Fig. 31 The 'oval' or, more properly, 'elliptical'-turning chuck. (*Holtz V*)

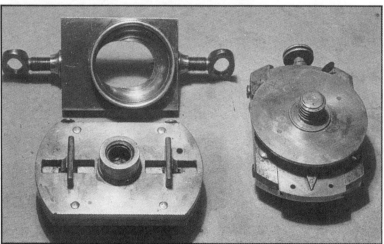

Fig. 32 The elliptical chuck from Holtzapffel No. 484, seen from the back, showing both the cam ring and the hard steel rubbing strips.

rotates, the forepart also will run coaxially. However, if the cam-ring is displaced sideways then the slide will move back and forth twice per revolution, thus describing an elliptical path at the nose 'a'. A very fine adjustment is given to the cam-ring by the operation of two screws (one of which is seen at 'm') which engage in the two centre-holes mentioned when we looked at the headstock, (see Fig. 17).

The chuck can be used both to turn elliptical works – boxes and the like (even the humble tool-handle!) – and also to generate surface patterns as in the case of the eccentric chuck.

### The Upright, Dome, or Spherical Chuck

This again is a very old device, shown in Fig. 33, which enables the work-chuck to be set at right angles to the mandrel axis. It is used chiefly as a work-setting device, as it runs badly out of balance when rotated at any speed. You will notice that the work can be indexed, and that also it can be moved vertically, to bring the part of the workpiece under cut up to lathe centre height. Using the headstock tangent screw it can, of course, be used (with the cutting frames) at any angle to the vertical. The photo shows the fluting of a dome.

Fig. 33 The 'dome', also known as an 'upright' or 'spherical' chuck, set up for fluting the top of a workpiece.

### The Rectilinear Chuck

This chuck was regarded by Holtzapffel as his most notable invention, though current practitioners might deny this, and insist that the 'eccentric cutting frame' is far more worthy of note. Fig. 34 shows my own, mounted on the lathe, and at first sight this looks exactly like an eccentric chuck. So it is, but it has a larger index wheel (120 teeth) and the slide can travel on *both* sides of the centre zero, a total of about four inches. It is far too heavy to use in rotation, and its purpose is to move the work relative to the cutter in both linear and rotary directions – actually, in two of each modes, taking the sliderest into account. It is, in effect, a 'milling slide' attached to the headstock. Again, we shall look at its 'powers' later, but Fig. 141 on page 160 will give you some idea of what a real expert (in this case, John Jacob Holtzapffel II in person) can do! The whole of this piece was made on one of his lathes!

There are many other forms of ornamental chuck produced during the 19th century, some made to the designs of amateurs, some part of the firm's normal production. Most are rare, and of limited application. The honest truth is that at one period 'Ingenuity triumphed over

Fig. 34 The rectilinear chuck. Note the much greater travel than that of Fig. 28.

Art' and the devices often owed more to the desire to explore some obscure facet of geometry than to the production of visually acceptable pieces. One of these, however, does deserve mention – the 'geometric' chuck – and we will have a look at it in Chapter 9.

## THE CUTTING FRAMES

The great difference between ornamental turning as practised in the past on the continent and those in this country – at least, for the last 140 years – lies in the expanded use of rotary cutting tools carried in the sliderest. One such device, the drilling spindle, was found even on the earliest lathes but the rest came later, largely due to the several generations of the Holtzapffel family. As it came first, we will look at the features of the drilling spindle before the others.

### The Ornamental Drills

Fig. 35 shows what can be done using a simple spear-pointed drill in conjunction with the indexing facility of the headstock. This example does involve other types of 'instrument' as well, but the delicacy of the

Fig. 35 The rim of this small vase has been decorated using the plain drills. (*Holtz V*)

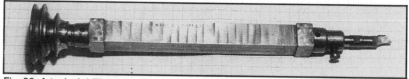

Fig. 36 A typical drilling spindle.

perforated vandykes is the chief attraction. Fig. 36 shows an actual spindle. The body, 9/16 inch square to fit the tool receptacle, carries the spindle between widely spaced cone bearings, steel on steel. The drills themselves have taper shanks to fit the socket at the front, and the two-speed pulley is driven from the lathe overhead. As usual, there is a problem! The drill shanks differ widely in their taper (there were no 'British Standards'!) and, unless they fit the spindle socket exactly, trouble will ensue.

The drills themselves range from simple spear points, in a range of diameters, to elaborately profiled form cutters; these also in varying sizes. Fig. 37 shows a typical 'set'. They are used for other purposes than drilling holes, decorative or otherwise. (See Fig. 37a.) I make much use of them for fluting and for making decorative beadings. Even small flycutters can be found! The instrument is very versatile and, perhaps, not used as much as it should be.

Fig. 37 A selection of drills. Each row of twelve has the same profile, but of a different size.

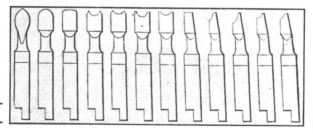

Fig. 37(a) Typical drill profiles. (*Holtz V*)

### The Vertical Cutting Frame

The name is deceptive, as the *spindle* is horizontal; it is the cutter which revolves in the vertical plane – Fig. 38. The shank (running out of the top of the photograph) fits the tool receptacle as usual. The tools, of two standard rectangular cross-sections, fit in the mortice of the spindle, secured by the small square-headed screw. (A packing trough is used with the smaller cutters.) The tools have various profiles, seen in Fig. 64 p. 66 and these profiles come in various sizes, like the drills. The *shape* is always known by the numbers seen in the engraving; the widths are quoted in hundredths of an inch, so that a No. 94 marked '5' would be flat-ended 0.05 inch wide. The angular cutters are marked with the angle to the longitudinal axis, which can be confusing. Both the No. 91 and the No. 92 seen in Fig. 64 would be marked '45'. This cutting frame (usually known as the 'VCF') has many applications which will be explored in later chapters, and I would regard it as an essential. Fortunately, it could be easily made, and could use round toolbits suitably ground if need be.

Fig. 38 The vertical cutting frame. (The cutter revolves in the vertical plane.)

Fig. 39 The horizontal cutting frame. The extension piece allows small cutters to be used at larger radius. (*Holtz V*)

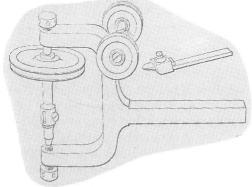

### The Horizontal Cutting Frame

This enables the cutter to rotate in the horizontal plane, Fig. 39. A pair of jockeys is needed in this design, to accept the drive from the overhead. It accepts the same tools as the VCF, but you will see there is an extension bar to enable it to cut at much larger radius. The pulley can, in fact, be changed for a smaller one when small radii and higher speeds are needed. It is very similar to a modern clock-gear cutting frame.

### The Universal Cutting Frame

This, as its name implies, can be used at any angle. Fig. 40 shows that the cutter drive assembly is carried on a spindle which passes through the square shank. This spindle has a calibrated protractor sector at the far end which enables the cutter to be set at any angle, including both horizontal and vertical. The nature of the construction demands

Fig. 40 The universal cutting frame of Holtzapffel design. It can be a little clumsy in use. (*Holtz V*)

the elaborate jockey-pulley arrangement, with a pair on either side. Frankly, it is not the happiest design! It performs its office beautifully, but it is *very* difficult to keep the drive cord on the jockeys. I prefer to use the *geared cutting frame* shown in Fig. 41. This is a Birch design, and very much more practical. (In fairness, while the UCF was designed over 150 years ago, the Birch was introduced in the late 1890s or early 1900s!) Many people express fears that the gears might cause chatter when making delicate patterns, but I have never found this a problem. I now use this instead of both the VCF and the HCF, as well as a truly 'universal' frame. The angular setting is, of course, necessary when cutting helical flutes or 'spirals' on the end face. One

Fig. 41 A later geared-type universal cutting frame by Birch. The design allows it to be used very close to the chuck. Longer arbors are provided, increasing its versatility.

advantage of the Birch type is that it can be fitted with extended spindles (there are four) so that you can work very close to any obstruction, impossible with that in Fig. 40.

### The Eccentric Cutting Frame

This, usually known as the 'ECF', is the most powerful (in its range of application) of all the cutting frames, even though the others are essential for certain work. Indeed, even a lathe with a simple head-stock (with dividing rings) and rudimentary sliderest, can produce very effective ornamental work with this cutting frame alone. Fig. 42 shows the construction, and you will see that it is basically an adjustable

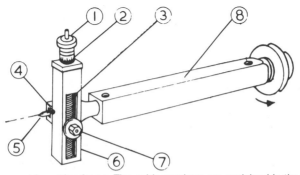

Fig. 42 The eccentric cutting frame. The guide numbers are explained in the text.

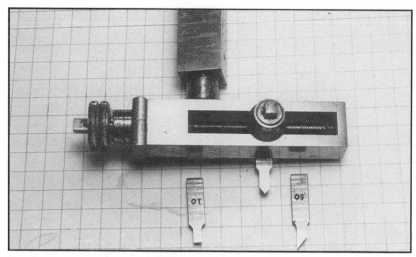

Fig. 43 A close-up of the Holtzapffel eccentric cutting frame, with some typical cutters.

flycutter. The spindle is similar to that on the drill (some makers provided an eccentric head to fit into the drilling spindle). The tool-holder (4) holds the top face of the cutter exactly in the plane of rotation of the spindle and can be set at the desired radius along the mortice in the head, (6), under the control of the fine thread screw (3). The head of this screw has a knob calibrated in hundredths of an inch, the divisions being fairly widely spaced so that setting to 0.001 inch is possible with care. The spindle is carried in the body, (8) which is a close fit to the tool receptacle of the sliderest. Fig. 43 is a close-up photograph of the head with three typical cutter-bits. (The background is marked in ¼-inch squares.)

If you refer back to the eccentric chuck you will realise that the machine must be stopped after every individual cut, so that the work may be indexed on the chuck nose. With this tool, however, the mandrel is *stationary*, and the cutter may be kept running (with due regard to safety!) while the headstock is indexed. A considerable saving in time – some patterns may require 300 different settings to completion! Further, the cutting frame (driven from the overhead) may be run very much faster, with consequent improvement in finish, and the tool runs very much cooler so that it stays sharp for longer. Its use is described in detail later, but it will be realised that the work is held in any ordinary work chuck. The radius of the circle to be cut is set on the head of the ECF, and the eccentricity, or pitch circle diameter, is set by the sliderest. The final advantage of this device is that it can be used on a conical face, or even on the circumference of the cylinder, impossible with the eccentric chuck. It can even be used to 'generate' geometric shapes, including the hemisphere. A powerful instrument indeed! Fig. 44 is a box lid the making of which required only the mandrel division circles and the ECF! (The making of this pattern is described in Chapter 4.)

Fig. 44 The famous 'fish' pattern, which is cut using the eccentric cutting frame. This cannot be made on the eccentric chuck.

## Special Cutting Frames

I do not intend to go into any detail at all on these, as they *are* special and though very fine work can be done with them they are rare, and demand more than a little imagination and expertise on the part of the user. But no account would be complete without mentioning one or two. The first is the *elliptical cutting frame* seen in Figs. 45 and 46. You will see that the cutting head of an eccentric cutting frame is gear-driven from a large pulley, D, the bearing of the ECF spindle being mounted *on* this pulley. You can also see that if the sector arm marked 'B' on the engraving is traversed sideways, the rotation of the ECF will be eccentric to that of the pulley. With suitable gear ratio (2/1) the tool in the cutting frame will describe an ellipse. Additional gears are sometimes provided enabling the device to cut three or four lobed figures. The first gear of the train – that nearest the mainplate – is stationary, and is attached to a spindle running through the shank to the rear. The worm indexing wheel is used to rotate this spindle, and hence the first gear, to establish the position of the 'start' of the incision, and to compensate for any changes which may be made to the position of the sector plate B as the pattern is cut.

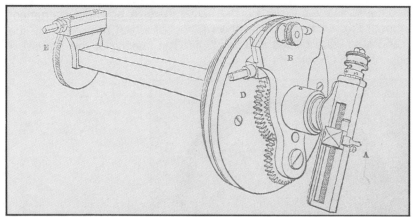

Fig. 45 The elliptical cutting frame. The gearing and other adjustments cause the tool to describe an elliptical path. (*Holtz V*)

Fig. 46 The author's elliptical cutting frame.

The *epicyclodal cutting frame* carries matters further still – Fig. 47. The principle is the same as that of the elliptical frame – a combination of two variable eccentricities, a variable radius, and a gear ratio – but the latter now allows considerable variation. My own has a set of 16 gears (plus two permanent) and a tumbler reverse pair. Even if linear adjustments are made only by one division at a time, something like a million variations of pattern are possible. (Although there are certain 'rules' which must be followed, otherwise the 'pattern' becomes a mere scribble!.) Fig. 47 shows my own in action, and Fig. 48 is an example of what can be achieved.

The *rose cutting frame* is an even rarer device, but does not, in my

Fig. 47 The author's epicycloidal frame. This one is made by Geo. Plant & Sons of Birmingham, and has a set of 16 gears, as well as four permanently fitted. Seen decorating the knob of the peppermill, Fig. 124.

Fig. 48 An extract from a Holtzapffel catalogue of about 1900, showing the type of pattern produced by Fig. 47.

view, rank as true 'ornamental turning' as the basic pattern is produced from templates or 'rosettes', the shape of which are not under the control of the user. Fig. 49 shows a few examples.

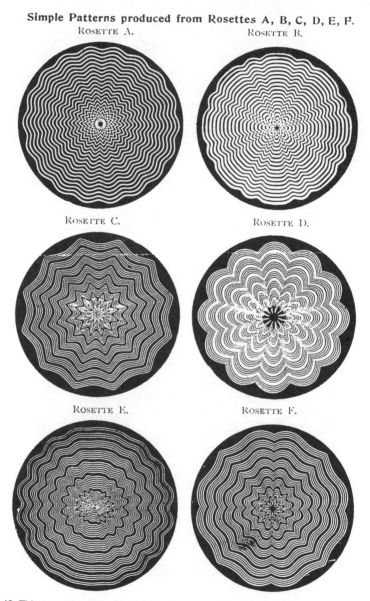

Simple Patterns produced from Rosettes A, B, C, D, E, F.

ROSETTE A.    ROSETTE B.

ROSETTE C.    ROSETTE D.

ROSETTE E.    ROSETTE F.

Fig. 49 This type of pattern is made by the *rose cutting frame* (not illustrated) which is a copying rather than a pattern-generating device.

Fig. 50 An early type of 'overhead', fitted to Holtzapffel No. 484. Despite its crude appearance it runs very well.

### Cutting Frame Drives

The 'overhead drive' is often regarded as the typical feature of an O.T. lathe. This is not the case, as many instrument lathes are so fitted for gear-cutting. However, some means of driving the drills and cutting frames is always needed and almost all ornamental lathes do have an overhead for this purpose. The usual form comprises a spindle mounted on a bracket carrying a pulley at one end to connect to the treadle and a drum in the centre from which a band can be taken to the cutting frame. Fig. 50 shows the early type on Holtz. No. 484 of 1805, the spindle being carried on a 'davit' attached to the end upright of the frame. The sprung bow applies some tension to the bands. The two 10-step pulleys are not for speed variation – that is effected by the treadler – but for coarse belt tensioning. Fig. 51 shows the later version of the same device, this time with a drum, which allows the drive band to move sideways as the cutting frame is traversed across the work.

The alternative is shown in Fig. 52, by Fenn, with the spindle carried on standards attached to the lathe backboard. The jockey arm and pulleys are recent additions.

Nowadays few practitioners use the overhead drum. Provided the centre distance is large enough, the pulleys can accept lateral deviation of the drive cord. Now that most lathes are motor driven, the usual arrangement is to set a small motor, perhaps with rubber feet, on the

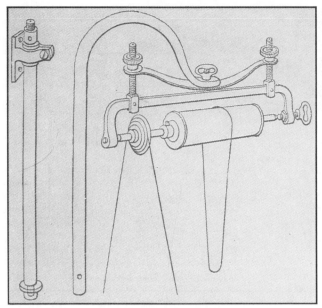

Fig. 51 The later type of 'davit' overhead. (*Holtz V*)

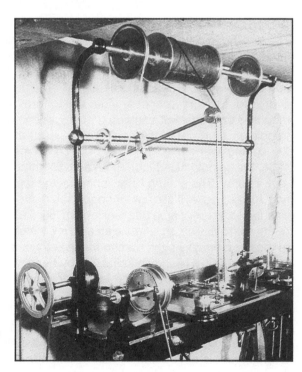

Fig. 52 Typical overhead of the 'shaft and standard' type; this one is by Fenn. Note the jockey pulleys.

Fig. 53 Cutting frame drive from a motor on the backboard. The cord runs over jockeys above, but in many applications a direct drive is possible. (The chuck seen is a 'die chuck'.)

backboard and drive the cutting frame through jockeys, as shown in Fig. 53. Coarse adjustment of tension is made on a jockey arm, and fine adjustment simply by pushing the motor about on the backboard. Speed variation can be obtained from cone pulleys, but I use a small DC motor fed through rectifiers and a variable transformer from the mains.

The drive cords were originally catgut bands. Small diameter leather belts with wire hook type fasteners or a glued scarf joint are better. The braided nylon cord, as used on electric light ceiling switches is good provided enough tension can be applied – it can be 'welded' with a lighted match. Those who can 'long splice' will find that 3 mm cotton drive ropes are ideal.

### Screw Threads and Spirals
'Spiral' is, of course, a misnomer; the proper name for the screw is 'helix' but long usage has given a mistaken respectability to the error, found in almost all books on ornamental turning!

Reference has already been made to the use of the traversing mandrel and screw guides. It should be remembered that almost the only need for screw threads in O.T. work is either in the making of chucks to fit the mandrel nose, or for joining together parts of complex works. The true ornamental turner will never use glue for this purpose if he can avoid it. Long threads are not needed and the travel of the mandrel – about an inch – is quite sufficient. The only point I would make here is to urge the retention of the treadle and a suitable drive cord, as this is the ideal way of operating the machine when using the guide bobbins. Unless, of course, the thread is cut using the vertical cutting frame, when hand drive is almost essential.

### The 'Spiral' Apparatus

This is used when long helices are to be cut – in effect it converts the machine into a screw-cutting lathe, but drives the feedscrew of the sliderest, not a leadscrew, the full length of the bed. Again, this is not specific to ornamental lathes as it was and is extensively used on instrument lathes.

Fig. 54 The so-called 'spiral apparatus', driving directly onto the feedscrew of the sliderest. (Holtz V)

There are many types. Fig. 54 shows the train of gears running from the front of the headstock directly to a gear on the free end of the mainslide screw, while in Fig. 55 the drive is from the back end of the headstock, with a bracket mounted on the bed to carry the drive shaft. (This is a real nuisance, as it means moving the headstock to make room for it.) On my own machine (which dates from 1897) the arrangement is much better – Fig. 56. The gear train lies at the back of the headstock but the drive to the sliderest is through a shaft which has both sliding and universal joints so that, within limits, neither the alignment nor the position of the sliderest is critical.

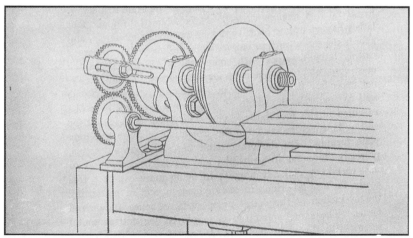

Fig. 55 In this design the spiral apparatus is attached to the rear of the headstock. Note the additional bearing bracket required. (*Holtz V*)

Fig. 56 A later type of spiral apparatus on Holtzapffel 2456. The shaft has both sliding and universal joints.

The system can be used to cut normal screw threads if need be – down to 96 tpi on mine – but the main purpose is for helical fluting and similar operations, with leads or pitches of up to eight inches. When used for this purpose the drive is taken *from* the sliderest feedscrew *to* the headstock, using the sliderest winch handle. The universal cutting frame is employed, so that the cutter can rotate in conformity with the lead angle of the helix.

An important feature, not seen either in the engravings or my photograph, is the indexing device shown in Fig. 57. This is keyed to the mandrel extension and carries the first wheel of the gear train. It has a click ratchet of 96 teeth, so that, having cut one flute, it is only necessary to disengage the ratchet, index round and relock, to cut the next. Without this device it is necessary to mark the wheels themselves (some are, in fact, so marked in any case) and to disengage the wheel train to change from one flute to the next.

With the arrangement in either Figs. 55 or 56 it is possible to fit a pair of bevel gears so that the sliderest may be set across the bed. It is then possible to cut true spirals on the end surface of the work. In most cases the bevels have curved faces to the teeth so that the rest may be set at other than a right angle, to cut a spiral on the cone. A more intriguing application is to use the apparatus in conjunction with the 'curvelinear' templates. I leave you to work out how to machine a segmented pineapple; no problem, I assure you!

Fig. 57 The indexing device of Fig. 56; this fits onto the mandrel and carries the first gear of the train.

### Combination of Apparatus

Of necessity in a book like this the various pieces of equipment must be treated in isolation. But much of the more 'advanced' (not necessarily the more aesthetically pleasing) work is done by the combination of chucks, chucks and cutting frames, or both associated with other equipment. Thus the eccentric chuck can be mounted on the elliptical, the dome chuck on the rectilinear, and so on. The production of a multi-start, eccentric, elliptical vase-shaped screw thread presents no problems at all – although the making of a nut to fit might take more time! The effective use of these combinations does need a fairly good knowledge of solid geometry, and a knowledge informed by some degree of artistic imagination, if visually acceptable works are to be produced.

### Conclusion

I have, of necessity, left out a number of accessories. In any gathering of ornamental turners you will always find a group hotly disputing the purpose for which some obscure device is intended. The manufacturers of the day were always willing to make *anything* for a customer (provided that he could pay for it) and were themselves far more innovative than we realise. In addition, many of the practitioners in the late 19th century were very skilful indeed, and made up special pieces of apparatus to suit their specific needs. It is just not possible to describe them all. I have left out 'Atkinson's Reciprocator' which allows the work to oscillate back and forth relative to the mandrel; the spherical sliderest, which enables perfect spheres to be produced; Beddow's patent 'combined epicycloidal, rose-cutting, eccentric cutting, drilling fluting and vertical cutting appliance'; Dumbleton's screw-cutting guide; the 'transfer chuck', and many others. Most of these are very rare. The use of others is so obvious that there is no need to explain them. Just one, however, is so fascinating – the 'geometric chuck' – that I have given this a chapter to itself later in the book.

Finally, you will notice that one very important matter seems to have been left out – the cutting tools themselves. True. But these are so important that they will be considered separately in the next chapter.

# 2 CUTTING TOOLS AND MATERIALS

The two subjects are dealt with together because the nature of the material does determine the shape and type of cutting tool needed. The *ornamental* turner is working on quite different types of stock compared to the spindle or bowl turner – ivory, ebony, blackwood etc – all of which are very close-grained and relatively hard. Some carry silicious inclusions and others are heavily impregnated with natural oils. While the conventional gouge and skew chisel *can* be used – and often are for reducing stock from the log – they cannot produce the finish or the effects that are essential in ornamental turning. There is the further point that while very little of the plain turners' work is done with the sliderest (indeed, the very basis of that craft lies in the use of offhand tools) the ornamental turner seldom uses his handrest. The two techniques are quite different, and a little consideration will show why.

In turning a softwood, or an open-grained hardwood like oak or mahogany the tool is ground to a fine cutting angle, typically 20 to 30 degrees, and presented to the work almost tangentially. The cutting action is very similar to that of a plane with the blade set at a flatter angle than usual. In place of the stock of the plane, the turning tool is guided by the rubbing of the bevel on the already turned surface – a fact which contributes to the finish, as this bevel acts as a burnisher. Unlike the plane, however, the turning tool has no 'sole' to control the chip formation. It does not, in fact, need one, as in turning all cutting is done *across* the grain. (When turning on the cylinder, that is; the situation is different when bowl turning.) This fact is not always appreciated, as the form of the chip is almost identical to that formed by a plane cutting *along* the grain. The combination of the action of the bevel and the high speed at which the cutting is carried out – very high in the case of softwoods – produces an acceptable finish despite the fact that the cutting edge is left pretty rough from the grindstone.

The conventional hardwoods behave in a similar fashion to the softwoods, though the turner may use a larger cutting angle. The tools need grinding more often but otherwise the technique used is the same. However, when very hard and dense woods are to be turned, the cutting edge is so rapidly destroyed that regrinding may take as long as the actual turning. The reason for this is not due to 'wear' in the accepted sense. African blackwood, for example, is less abrasive than oak or ash. But the density, and the higher shear strength across the grain means that more work is done in the cutting, and this work all appears as *heat* at the cutting edge. Some will be carried away by the chip, but not much, as the specific heat of timber is low. Some may pass into the workpiece but, again, this will not be much; quite apart from the low specific heat, wood is a good heat insulator. Almost the whole of the work done appears as heat *at the tool point*. This means that the tip can get very hot, the metal is softened, and the tip either chips off or wears away very quickly.

The remedy is twofold. First, the cutting speed is reduced. This reduces the *rate* of heat release and (oversimplifying the situation a little) gives the heat a better chance of passing down to the tool shank without too high a temperature at the tip. Unfortunately this reduction in speed changes the very nature of the cutting action and the finish will suffer. The second remedy is to increase the cutting angle (Fig. 58a shows a few tool definitions) to between 60 and 80 degrees instead of the plain turner's 20 to 30 degrees. (At 40 degrees it might be possible to use the 'rubbing bevel' technique but not at anything much greater.)

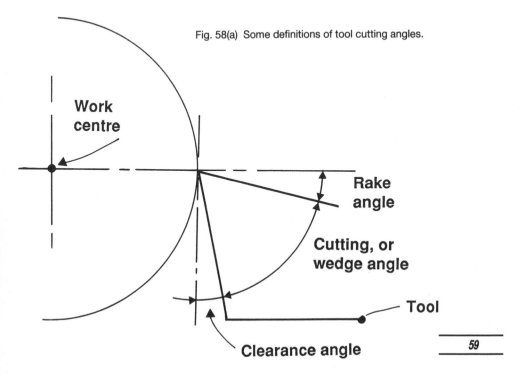

Fig. 58(a)  Some definitions of tool cutting angles.

**Work centre**

**Rake angle**

**Cutting, or wedge angle**

**Tool**

**Clearance angle**

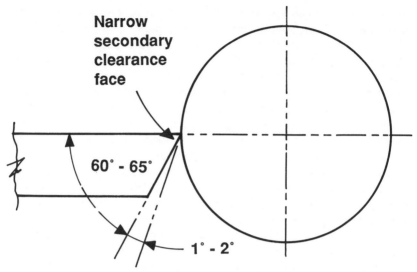

**Narrow secondary clearance face**

60° - 65°

1° - 2°

Fig. 58(b) The type of cutting edge used for ivory and exotic woods. The same angles can be used for brass.

There is a further change, too. When the bevel is rubbing in softwood turning, the top face of the tool (the 'rake' angle in Fig. 58a) is almost tangential to the workpiece. The increase in cutting angle makes this impossible – we must preserve a reasonable front clearance to the tool. The combined effect is to impose not only a change of technique but also a change in the actual cutting action. The chip is now formed *in pure shear* rather than the mainly slicing action of the gouge or chisel. The tool is set with zero rake – the top face is held radial to the centre of rotation instead of being almost tangential. The fibres are sheared, just as when turning metal. The combination of lower cutting speed, thicker tool profile, and the shearing action reduces the tip temperature to an acceptable figure. However, we do have to pay a price. If the same tool-sharpening technique is used the finish will be very poor indeed. With this type of tool, the cut surface will be a replica in negative of the surface of the tool, and any grinding marks will appear on the work. As ornamental turning relies, for a large part of its effect, on the reflections from the surface, especially in the case of incised patterns, this is important. It is not possible to achieve this effect by subsequent abrasive polishing – a process which is anathema to the ornamental turning even if it *were* possible to polish some of the incised patterns you will see later in the book.

This use of zero rake tools is often a matter of great controversy in plain turning circles. Spindle or bowl turners assert that only a chisel or gouge will 'cut wood as it likes to be cut' and deride the zero rake tool as a mere 'scraper'. I doubt very much whether wood *ever* 'likes

Fig. 59 This photograph of a tool cutting Brazilian rosewood on the endgrain shows that these tools do produce 'long and curly' chips. Definitely *not* scraping!

to be cut' whatever tool is used, but Fig. 59 shows quite clearly that a tool with zero top rake and a cutting angle of about 70 degrees does produce 'curly chips' even when, as in the photo, it is attacking the endgrain. I have measured such chips as much as five feet long when turning ivory and almost as long with boxwood. It is, however, vital that the tool be *really* sharp, and we shall return to that later.

There is one other matter which must be mentioned before leaving all these generalities. It is not at all uncommon for a cutting-frame tool to make several hundred cuts before it can be removed for resharpening. Many tools have a very complex planform, which means that they can be sharpened only on the top face. Any excessive wear which affected the form of the tool could be very serious. (One pair of tools I have seen produced, when used successively, a profile of Queen Victoria!) The tool cutting edge is, therefore, *the* paramount concern of the ornamental turner. As, of course, it should be for all turners, whatever their medium. The lathe is, after all, no more than a device for presenting the tool to the workpiece, and the most sophisticated Numerically Controlled Machining Centre is worthless scrap if the tool

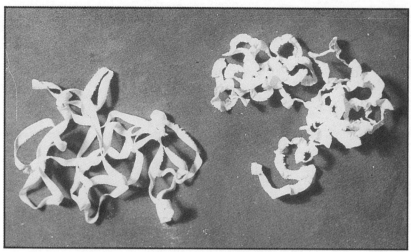

Fig. 59(a) 'Long and curly' chips from an ivory workpiece.

point is defective. The casual approach of many turners to the care and sharpening of their cutting tools is much to be regretted.

### Types of Tool

As already noticed, all types of tool used in the O.T. machine are held in the same 'receptacle' (with or without adaptors) and will all find their cutting edges at centre height until they become damaged or too worn. There will, of course, be differences between makes, but that is to be expected. There are three basic types, four if we include the drills.

### Heavy Tools

These all have a square shank which fits the tool receptacle, $\frac{9}{16}$ or $\frac{5}{8}$ inch square, and about five or six inches overall length. Fig. 60 shows a typical set, but Nos. 155, 161 and 162 are for metal turning. (O.T. lathes *are* used on metal, and, of course, cup chucks and backplates must be machined.) The use of most of these will be fairly clear, but note the deep section of the parting tool, No. 156. These tools are, as the name suggests, mainly for heavy work but their long projection and stiff form enables the turner to get at awkward parts of the work, especially when close to the chuck. There are many special shapes. Fig. 61 is a curved trepanning tool, for taking out the interior of hollow work. When using ivory especially, every scrap of material is of value. Fig. 62 is a gouge tool with renewable insert, which can remove material very quickly indeed. I use it when converting from the log.

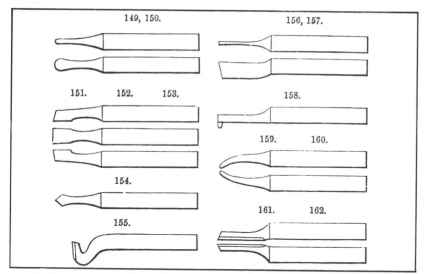

149, 150.     156, 157.

151.    152.    153.     158.

    159.    160.

154.

    161.    162.

155.

Fig. 60 Typical 'heavy' sliderest tools. These can be used for decoration in awkward places, as well as for 'roughing'. (*Holtz V*)

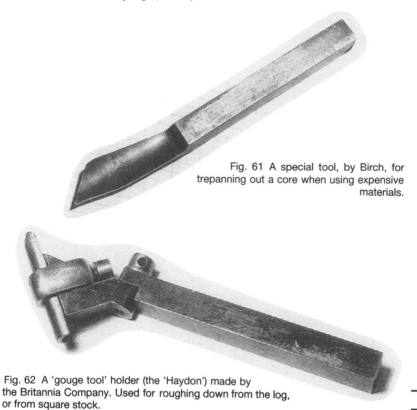

Fig. 61 A special tool, by Birch, for trepanning out a core when using expensive materials.

Fig. 62 A 'gouge tool' holder (the 'Haydon') made by the Britannia Company. Used for roughing down from the log, or from square stock.

## Small Sliderest Tools

These form the main tool system and have shanks of section which vary from maker to maker, but most are more or less $\frac{11}{32}$ inch wide × $\frac{5}{32}$ inch thick. They are held in a brass 'toolboat' which fits inside the topslide tool receptacle and Fig. 63 shows a typical range. At (a) are the common turning tools. Those at (b) are 'decorating' tools, and a complete set would include several widths of each profile. The row at (c) are 'specials' (although there would, of course, be boring tools in the normal range). The 'specials' can, literally, be any shape you please. No. 43 (the tools are all known by their numbers) is interesting. It is used for the making of rings like the old-fashioned curtain ring. Having machined a hollow tube of the correct dimension, this tool is applied to the outside and produces a semicircular bead all round. The opposite face of the tool is then applied to the inside of the tube, and will neatly part off a ring of true circular cross-section. Nos. 44 to 47 are shaped to the classical forms of architectural column plinths etc. Allowing for the differing widths, and angles of the bevel tools, there may be 180 tools in a 'set', but many are never used at all.

The material of these tools is high-carbon steel of great purity, with no alloying elements at all. One specimen I had tested revealed only the barest trace of silicon, and that far too small to be measured. They

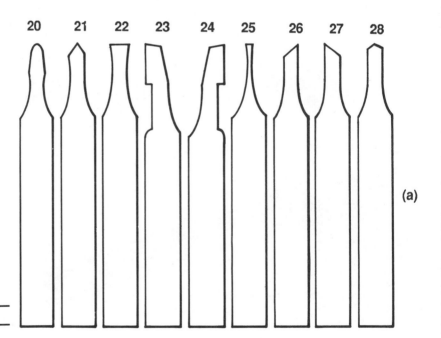

20    21    22    23    24    25    26    27    28

(a)

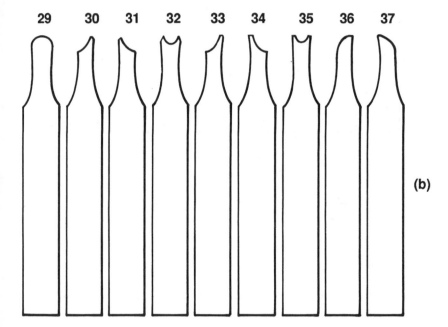

Fig. 63 The normal sliderest tools. Those at (a) are for general turning (though No. 21 can be used for decoration); (b) are for forming circumferential patterns and (c) are boring and special form tools. Most come in grades of widths and (where appropriate) angles. The tools are known by their number, and the width or angle as the case may be. (*Holtz V*)

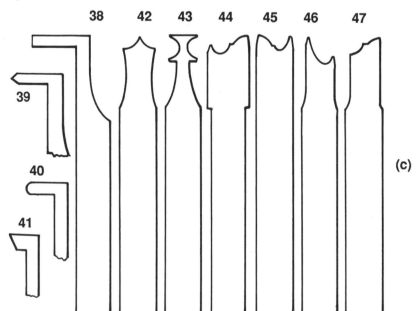

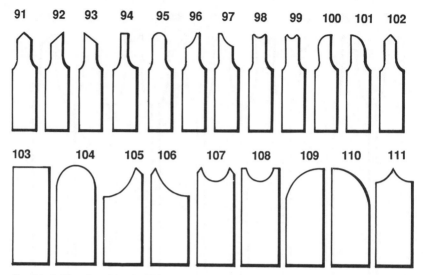

Fig. 64 Cutting frame tools. There are two shank sizes, but the smaller ones are the most used. Like the sliderest tools they come in various sizes and angles. (*Holtz V*)

have been tempered to about 850 on the Vickers Diamond Pyramid machine (65 on Rockwell 'C'). These figures can readily be obtained with modern materials but most users seem to agree that these old tools have a longer life. More important, perhaps, is what appears to be a very fine grain size, which allows the cutting edge to be lapped to a high polish. Some of the tools, notably No. 20, are used a great deal, with much resharpening. The tempering has been done in the classical fashion, from the shank forwards, so that the hardness can drop quite rapidly away from the point. Any tool more than $\frac{3}{16}$ inch shorter than when new is likely to return a hardness down to perhaps 700 VDP.

### Cutting Frame Tools

Some of these have the same cross-section as the sliderest tools, although they are shorter, but most are smaller, with shanks 0.210 × 0.110 inch, whatever the maker. Fig. 64 shows the common shapes, the smaller size having the larger range. Although the range of planforms is lower than for the sliderest tools the increments of angle of, for example, Nos. 91 to 93 are much smaller (about 5 degrees) and the widths or radii of others have increments of 0.01 inches. This means that a complete set might include 300 or more cutters. There is no need to be dismayed, however, as I managed for some years with one each of Nos. 91, 92 and 93 and three of No. 94 of different widths!

### Ornamental Drills

As already noticed, these may have several forms of taper shanks, depending both on the maker and when they were made. Some by Holtzapffel had parallel shanks, and were held in the drill spindle with a setscrew. The shapes are legion, and my Evans drill cabinet has space for 324 of the smaller type (they come in two or three body sizes). Fig. 37a, p. 42 shows a few typical profiles. The absence of some shapes and sizes is not very important, though, as you just design your fluting or beading to suit what is available. Fig. 65 shows a typical 'sloping top cabinet' containing sliderest tools at the top, cutting frame tools in the middle drawer and drills at the bottom.

### Choice of Cutter

From what has gone before it follows that the ornamental turner of the last century would often be spoiled for choice in selecting a cutter – he might well have over 1000 to choose from if he could afford a full outfit. The fact that cabinets such as Fig. 65 still appear with most of the cutters unused emphasises this! However, even in those days these tools were not cheap – 30 shillings (£1.50, or $6 at the then rate of exchange) a dozen in 1912 – so that most turners were content, as we are today, with fewer. I find that I use most of those shown at

Fig. 65 The tool cabinet. Sliderest tools in the top, cutting frame tools in the upper drawer, and drills in the lower.

Fig. 63a, together with two rather special parting tools; about three sizes of each of Nos. 30 to 37 in Fig. 63b and several boring tools in the sliderest (as well as a few of the 'heavy' type). In the cutting frames almost all my work is done with a few of No. 91 to 93, three sizes of the flat tool No. 94, and a couple each of Nos. 95, 98 and 99 in Fig. 64, while half a dozen drills serve all my needs. I do have a lot more, and use many, but only on rare occasions. As Holtzapffel himself says more than once in his books, the basis of the art lies more in 'restraint' rather than in enthusiastic proliferation of decoration.

### Making Cutters

I do not propose to go into detail on the hardening and tempering of these tools, as there is a special section in my book *Hardening and Tempering* (also published by Argus Books) which deals specifically with tools for ornamental turning. However, a few words may not be out of place. Silver steel is an acceptable material, but it is becoming increasingly difficult to obtain in other than round bar. A good substitute is *file steel*, but this must be *thoroughly* annealed before shaping and rehardening, and it is vital not only that the teeth be removed, but also at least $\frac{1}{32}$ inch of the material below the teeth, as the act of cutting them has an effect well below the surface. The best type to use are large square files, as these have plenty of metal in them and can be obtained (free!) from blacksmiths' and welders' scrap bins! The other matter I would emphasise, although I deal with it in detail in the book just mentioned, is the tempering. For cutting frame tools I would not temper higher than 100 to 120 degrees C, and not more than 150 degrees C for the smaller sliderest tools; indeed, boiling water will do for the point of these too, but you may have to let the shank down more – to the pale straw colour with *no* colour at all showing within $\frac{3}{8}$ inch of the tool point.

### Tool Sharpening

Assuming a new tool is being made, or an old one is to be altered the shape can be formed in the conventional manner on a grinding wheel. It is a good practice to use a soft wheel running slowly with continuous flow of water rather than the high-speed double-ended tool grinder and water pot. If this type is all that is available, I prefer to tackle several tools at the same time so that I can take just a little off each in turn and allow them to cool naturally. 'Thermal shock' is as bad for tools as it is for people!

The grinding marks must then be removed completely on an oilstone, finishing with fine India. As a rule, care and the frequent use of a protractor square is all that is needed at this stage. The object of the process so far is to remove all traces of grinding marks, to approach the correct angles, and (if the tool has just been hardened) to remove any slight decarbonised surface at the cutting edge. It follows that with a new tool the top surface must also be stoned, but care must be taken to keep it dead flat.

The tool can now be finished. A hard Arkansas oilstone is needed, although I find that the Carborundum Company's 'Superfine White' type CF7 oilstone does very well. Others use 'Tam o' Shanta' water stone. Both the clearance face and the top must be treated. Finally, the secondary clearance angle is made (see Fig. 58b) by lapping the face on a flat iron surface with rouge and oil. This facet can be quite narrow, and should not exceed about one eighth of the thickness of the tool in width. All this work can be done 'offhand', perhaps with the aid of an angled block to maintain the profiles accurately, but for really precise work, especially on the small cutting frame tools, the *Goniostat* should be used if available. These are not rare (though I fear that many now grace mantelpieces as 'decoration') and a simple one can easily be made. Fig. 66 shows an elaborate one by Holtzapffel. The tool is held in the clamp at the front, usually in an adaptor, as the slot is made to accept the largest sliderest tools. This holder can be set over at an angle sideways either way, and clamped by a bolt passing through the circular slot. It can also be set to the clearance angle – in the engraving

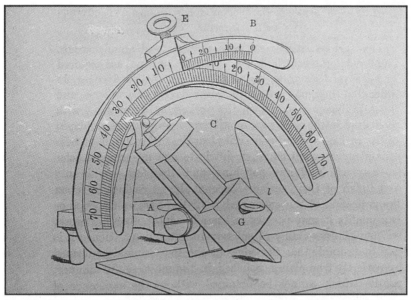

Fig. 66 The 'goniostat' for sharpening both sliderest and cutting frame tools. Its use is explained in the text. (*Holtz V*)

this is 30 degrees – and locked. The projection of the tool is adjusted so that when set on a flat surface the base also sits flat, supported on the two pegs at the back and the clearance face of the tool. The latter rests on a lapping plate and the whole instrument is moved about to lap the face of the tool.

The complete outfit, Fig. 67 (by Birch), has three such laps, as shallow drawers which can be withdrawn from the cabinet. The first carries a hard Arkansas slip; the second a brass plate which is used with very finely ground Arkansas stone dust, and the third plate is of iron, used with rouge powder – all, of course, with oil, usually Neatsfoot, though I find that '3 in 1' is easier to use. After dealing with the clearance face, the top of the tool is then treated, taking the *greatest* care to keep it dead flat on the lapping plate. It is here that many tools lose their cutting edge as, over the years, there is a tendency for it to become convex on top.

Fig. 67 The author's goniostat outfit by Birch. The cabinet contains oil and lapping powders, while the lapping plates are integral with the drawers.

Fig. 68 The sharpening apparatus for concave tools. The pulley is screwed onto the mandrel nose. It is unfortunate that both work and sliderest must be removed in order to sharpen a tool!

It is not, as a rule, necessary to go through the whole of this process every time. Most normal restoration will be done with no more than a quick rub on the iron lap and, after a longer period of use, on the brass and then iron, but I have gone through the whole to give a complete picture. I should, however, add that many of the most expert practitioners scorn the use of the Goniostat, doing almost all their resharpening by freehand methods. This is fair enough – for the expert! But even so, it helps to know what you are aiming at. Without the Goniostat, or some simpler angle-setting device (which is what the word means!) It is very difficult to get the two sides of a vee tool equally disposed, or the end of a flat tool square across. For *roughing* tools, of course, an edge finished on the fine India should suffice. And for the normal turning tools, including those for facing and boring, the finish obtained from the Arkansas or the 'Fine White' is quite adequate, although I always form the secondary bevel.

*Curved tools* are not so easy. Concaves, like Nos. 30, 32 or 98 etc, can be reformed using a fine conical Arkansas slipstone (a No. 27 'point') or a round edged gouge slip. If it is necessary to carry things further, then a small conical brass 'point' can be made in a holder to fit the lathe mandrel (or a flexible shaft unit, if available) and charged with oilstone dust or rouge. A fairly complex outfit specifically for this purpose was offered by most O.T. lathe makers (Fig. 68) and very nice too. However, it has the grave disadvantage that you have to take down the work already in the machine to use it, and it is just when you are in the middle of a job that you find the cutter needs attention! (Although, of course, you *ought* always to retouch all tools as soon as they are finished with!)

*Convex tools* are not so difficult, and I find that offhand methods are quite adequate, using the lapping plates belonging to the Goniostat. Care is needed to avoid forming flats, but that is all. A *very* complex device was offered by Evans and Holtzapffel which enabled such tools to be formed and sharpened to an exact radius, but it is questionable whether this (or even Fig. 68) is really worthwhile.

To the spindle or bowl turner accustomed to softwoods these processes may seem to be unduly pernickety! Indeed, at least one eminent offhand ('plain') turner has gone into print to say that an edge straight from the grinder will give a finish *better* than one which has been shown to an oilstone. This may be true when turning coarse-grained woods (although I very much doubt it) but even then the presence of the rubbing bevel contributes as much to the finish as does the tool edge. The bowl turner seems to go further, one authority recommending the raising of a feather edge to the tool by 'ticketing'! This may well remove stock faster, but it is noticeable that he then went on to give much attention to the use of the subsequent abrasive polishing that was necessary. For the ornamental turner this is just not on. It is quite impossible to 'polish' incised decoration. And while it *is* possible to polish an undecorated surface, any abrasive left in the grain would destroy the cutting edge of tools subsequently used very quickly. The most that we can do is to 'raise a shine' on undecorated surfaces using the parent wood shavings or, in the case of ivory, whiting and water (or even Brasso). We must always aim for a reflective tool finish, and this can never be better than the finish on the cutting edge of the tool.

## MATERIALS

To cover this in any detail would be very difficult. Not the least of the problems is availability. Many of the woods formerly used have been overcropped and others have been found to be more profitable when converted into veneer, so that the species can no longer be found 'in the block'. However, the situation is not desperate. Plenty of suitable material is still to be had, although it may be necessary to tailor the size of the work to suit what can be had. The primary requirement is that of a dense, very close and uniform grain – a total absence of grain would be the ideal cutting material, if somewhat uninteresting! This implies timber from trees of very slow growth.

*Ivory* is, of course, the classic material. Quite apart from its colour and appearance, it possesses all the attributes which make it a first-class turning material. Though relatively hard it machines very freely at moderate speeds, and a highly reflective surface is obtained from 'tool finish' without the need for any subsequent polishing, provided, of course, that the tools themselves have a high finish. Unfortunately the demand for ivory for purposes other than ornamental turning has not only pushed up the price to a prohibitive level for most of us, but has also led to a wholesale slaughter of elephants. I deal with this aspect in some detail in the section on 'Conservation' (page 79), but clearly we must seek an alternative that does not put these magnificent animals at risk. There is, of course, a certain amount of ivory which has been in private hands for many years – some relics from earlier generations of turners, others in the form of 'trophies' – and we can use this without any qualms. (Though I should warn readers that a tusk which has been displayed for decades over the fireplace is likely to have deteriorated very badly and will almost certainly be cracked.) What else can we do?

The first alternative is to change the design of the objects we make. For example, instead of making a box entirely of ivory, it can be made of a darker wood, perhaps embellished with ivory rings. Almost all the objects shown in Chapter 7 could be made equally well of lignum-vitae or blackwood. That shown in Figs. 128–132 (page 152), for example, could be made of lignum for the body, blackwood for the lid and base, with only the 'fish' pattern of ivory.

The second alternative is to seek other materials with a similar appearance.

**Mammoth Tusk** is an alternative that seldom comes to mind! However, it is available in large quantities in Siberia and other parts of the USSR and can be imported without difficulty (this must however be done through ivory merchants, as a shipment of less than a ton or so is not economical). Though sometimes known as 'fossil' ivory, a truer description would be 'deep frozen' and, as the tusks have lain at sub-zero temperatures for thousands of years, some deterioration is to be expected. I have recently acquired a piece taken from the centre of a tusk, which is oval and about 4½ inches × 5 inches. It exhibits what I can only call 'onionisation': there is a number of circumferential cracks, three running part way round and one complete. These are similar to those occasionally found in African ivory, but are filled with a white powder. Most of the tusk shows a few tiny cracks through the bark, but over one sector there has evidently been some very ancient damage, causing four radial cracks about an inch deep; a sector of the surface is missing over about 60 degrees. This damage has evidently allowed both water and sand to intrude, and subsequent freezing has opened up both the radial and the circumferential cracks in the vicinity. There is a section in the centre, a little over two inches in diameter, which is quite sound.

Rather depressing! However, it machines very well indeed, taking a reflective surface from the tool and responding to polishing with its own shavings just like African ivory. The shavings come off as 'curly chips' but are more brittle. The white inclusions cause no problems, but the few milligrams of Siberian tundra present will blunt the tool rapidly – I overcame this by tapping the piece gently with a small nylon hammer, when almost all fell out. The colour is a very pleasing cream, and the 'cross-hatching' pattern found in Ugandan ivory is present in the endgrain, together with some attractive radial striations of slightly darker colour in the centre. The 'nerve' is a mere dot. The bark is, perhaps, slightly thicker and rather harder than that from an elephant tusk of the same size, but it is difficult to judge as it has been coated for export with a dark varnish making it difficult to establish the colour. I have not experimented with cutting speeds, since it responded well to those I would normally use for elephant tusk. Looking at this piece I would say that had there been no initial damage on the outside – possibly thousands of years ago – there would have been no sandy inclusions, but the circumferential cracks might have prevented the piece from being used as a block.

However, we know that a great deal, if not the majority, of turned and carved artefacts made in Russia are of mammoth ivory, so it may well be that only their rejects are exported. My conclusion is that the sound sections are the equal of African elephant tusk, both in appearance and ease of working, and some might prefer it, especially if the almost imperceptible nerve in my piece is typical. I shall be able to use the centre cylinder of this piece. Much of the rest may be usable by cutting into sections and cementing together, while the residue will certainly be suitable for such items as pins or lace bobbins.

*Synthetic Ivory* comes in a number of forms – at one time **Xylonite** was used, though somewhat harsh if not carefully treated. I have tried three. The first is a material called CORIAN – I do not know the composition. It machines very well, and will leave a reflective surface from the tool almost as good as that of ivory, although some experimentation with cutting speed may be needed. It is very nearly the correct colour, but rather bland and characterless – there are no 'shades' as with true ivory and it is without grain on the endface.

A cast polyester resin known as PLC/3374/LA, marketed by GPS Agencies of Chichester, is cleverly blended with some form of random dye, which provides the 'character' lacking in corian, although there is still no pattern within the endgrain. It machines very well indeed, especially if cut at high speed, and I found no problems with the usual 'zero rake' cutting tools normally used for ornamental work. It accepts incised decoration readily, but though the tool finish is excellent it does not form a desired reflective surface. Decorative features which can be polished come up very well and artefacts carrying decoration which can be buffed is almost indistinguishable from genuine ivory. It might be possible with care to polish a deep-cut barleycorn pattern and shallow-cut basketwork, but not the more delicate tartan and its derivatives, since these would tend to lose the sharp edges. The problem lies, I am told, with the effects of the dyes, for the same firm also market what they call PLAIN IVORY SUBSTITUTE, which is the identical cast resin without the dye. This does give a reflective surface, especially if cut at higher speeds than normal for ivory, but is, of course, without the delicate shading found on African ivory (I understand however that it is a very close match to the so-called 'Indian' ivory much used by ivory carvers in the East).

It is, of course, necessary to experiment when using any new material and as demand from turners increases, the manufacturers of all these synthetic materials will come to pay attention to the special needs. (Most of the synthetics have been developed to suit the mass production of buttons and costume jewellery.) All that can be said at present is that these materials *can* be an acceptable substitute where colour and machining qualities are concerned. I shall be using them in future, keeping my small stock of ivory (all of which is many years old) for those cases where the importance of the subject justifies its use. I shall also be keeping an eye open for old ivory billiard balls; these, if not cracked through age or ill-usage, were made from the finest African ivory then available (none will be less than fifty years old). However, no-one who has any feeling at all for the preservation of the elephant should consider the purchase of any **NEW** tusks (see p. 79).

*Boxwood* is a turning material beyond reproach if of good quality. It is unfortunate that it picks up dirt so badly, so that decorated work must be varnished or lacquered, but it takes the finest detail. (It was, of course, used over the centuries for printer's blocks.) The English and Scottish box is a little prone to splits and shakes and can sometimes behave in an alarming manner if subjected to extremes of temperature. Unfortunately the Turkish and Persian varieties, once imported in great quantities for the making of boxwood mallets and scale rules, are not so freely available as they once were. But boxwood remains the ornamental turners' best friend, for they can use it to work out the settings and procedures, and check the design, before proceeding on more exotic wood or ivory. In addition, it is the ideal material for the making of both block and wood spring chucks.

**African blackwood** makes a superb contrast to ivory, and it is not surprising that much is imported as 'Chessman Blocks'. At its best it is jet black, but even the less dark specimens will darken with age. It contains an essential oil, which greatly facilitates turning. It is unfortunate that, in growth, the tree develops internal cavities and there may sometimes be serious growth shakes, so that the conversion factor from the log is rather poor. Even more unfortunate is the fact that much is now converted in the forest into 'sticks' for the manufacture of bagpipes and chessmen etc, so that large pieces are relatively rare. However, it is still (at time of writing) being imported in the log. The wood takes decoration equally well on the endgrain as on the plankway, and is rather more stable than many woods. It is rather expensive.

**Holly** is a whitewood with most of the desired characteristics, being close-grained and hard when seasoned. Quite white, if properly treated when felled, it is a good foil to blackwood. *Home* seasoning is very difficult as the shrinkage rates in the three planes are very different and shakes (splits) are almost inevitable. It is always prudent when accepting holly, even from the merchants if sawn, to turn it down nearly to the designed diameter as soon as possible, for often an apparently sound piece will develop a shake shortly after the first cut.

**Lignum-vitae** is easily obtainable, both in the log and as blocks. The 'engineering quality' is rather more expensive but well worth the price for important works. The ordinary lignum is used for the making of bowls woods and foundry tools; worn out 'woods' are a useful source if not badly split. The pale sapwood is slightly more open on the endgrain than the heartwood but turns well, the two colours making an agreeable contrast if the junction can be arranged to appear in the right place on the work. In the log it can be obtained in diameters up to 16 or 18 inches, although there is a risk of heart-shakes. Like blackwood it contains an essential oil, turns very well indeed and will accept deep-cut decoration. I find it useful, too, for chucks and faceplates, as it is very stable.

**Ebony** will take decoration very well on the endgrain and tolerably well on the cylinder, but it comes in a number of varieties, some jet black, ranging down to a greeny-black in colour. At its best, it is almost the equal of blackwood in appearance. The main problem is that it often contains silicious inclusions, carried up with the sap and crystallising out between the fibres – sometimes even filling quite large cracks. This is very damaging to the tools. However, it is usually possible to detect these when cross-sawing, and then to reduce the block to several smaller ones, avoiding the inclusions. At its best, it is a very fine wood indeed if you can accept the reduced tool life in turning it, and an ornamentally turned ebony box can be a real delight.

*Camwood* is a hard, red – very red when newly cut – wood which takes good decoration on the endgrain but is a trifle coarse plankways – it is one of the few woods which I find does need abrasive polishing on the cylinder occasionally, but it turns well. It is often confused with **padauk** which is similar in colour but inferior in performance. Many people are put off by the harsh red colour when newly cut but, after exposure to the air for a while, it takes a very rich tint which matures even more with age.

*Kingwood* was, at one time, very much sought after for ornamental turning – it still is, for that matter, but is very rare nowadays. It has a very fine appearance indeed and some would say that it is a pity to decorate it, but if used with discretion surface decoration can be very effective indeed.

*Brazilian rosewood* is a superb variety of the species and turns exceptionally well. However, it is such a beautiful material in itself that any ornamental work should be confined to 'ornament of form' rather than of pattern – though very discrete incised patterns on the endgrain are permissible. Again, it is difficult to come by in any reasonable size, as most of it is imported in sticks for the making of recorders and the like in school workshops. However, with a little care, larger sizes can be had by gluing the sticks together, with due regard to the pattern in the grain. It is far superior to the ordinary Indian rosewood.

*Fruitwoods* – apple, pear, plum, cherry, and even damson – have the two merits of being indigenous and available, although here again the change in orchard practice means that large pieces will soon be very rare. The prudent turner will keep an eye open for 'the old apple tree' and go into action immediately if the wind (or the chainsaw) brings it down. Pear is best for detail, and apple (well seasoned) is very hard, once being the favourite for the teeth in mill gearing. Some of the exotic fruits, like apricot and peach, are mentioned in early works but hardly likely to be available today.

*Yew* is a wood seldom mentioned in works on ornamental turnery but, provided that it is selected and turned with care (best reduced to the cylinder while still 'wet'), it can be very attractive. Not until the piece is nearly finished can a decision be made about applied decoration, as the grain – or, rather, the 'rings of colour' – may either forbid or demand some machined embellishment. I find it very attractive for making oval boxes.

*Partridge wood* is very hard indeed – in fact, if cut with a bandsaw at normal speed you may well lose the edge of the teeth at the first cut, and it is murder on plane-irons! It machines well, however, if the speed is kept within reason. Its attraction springs from the extraordinary configuration of the grain which, if cut on the right plane, resembles the feathers of a partridge. More than the most restrained decoration is inappropriate, but as seen on the pepper mill on Fig. 121 page 147, it makes an admirable material for the bodies of pieces carrying decorated parts made from other species.

### Other Materials

There are many materials, some known for centuries as 'ornamental turning woods' which I have not mentioned, as the likelihood of any appearing today is remote (even if they could now be identified). Of the 'oddities' I should, perhaps, mention **hippopotamus tooth**, which does appear as a curio at auctions occasionally. This has an enamel so hard that it can be used to true up a grindstone, but the dentine inside turns like ivory. If sectors can be cut off and opened these can be made into pendants, with an incised pattern on the soft face. **Jet** can be turned, though that picked up from the sea is likely to be very fragile; it must be 'mined' jet – but please don't go scaling any cliffs to get at it! It must be turned at very low speed – the so-called jet-turners of Whitby relied more on abrasive wheels to make their pieces. **Coconut shells** will take excellent decoration if they are sufficiently symmetrical and suitable workholding chucks can be devised. **Oxhorn** and **buffalo horn** make superb pieces, although ornament must be of form, not decoration. The appearance while turning is depressing (and the smell atrocious) but when finally buffed the result is superb. I use buffalo for handles on my lathes (See Fig. 20, page 28).

It will be observed that I have not mentioned any of the usual 'furniture' woods. This is because where they are suitable for turning, any form of decoration would be out of place. They are 'chisel and gouge' woods in the main. One, of which I am very fond, is **Cocobolo-wood** – a timber which the yard man told me 'the log had more "O"s than wood in it'. Of the rosewood family it is quite superb for 'form and shape' pieces (e.g the base of a decorated candlestick), but goggles and face-mask, please, or, preferably, a respirator, for it is one of the more virulent 'allergy' woods!

I must mention modern plastics. Many recoil at the idea of using them, but *provided the design is adapted*, work in these materials can be more than acceptable. Some now available are almost indistinguishable from ivory – and can even deceive the experts. Those which are transparent can be decorated on the obverse, so that the pattern is seen *through* the piece, and those with the necessary skill and design capability will cut a pattern on *both* sides so that each complements the other. Artefacts made from self-coloured materials can also be attractive but again, provided the design is appropriate, and not a mere modern replica of traditional form. The cast resin referred to on page 74, supplied by GPS Agencies Ltd, is available in a wide variety of forms simulating tortoishell, mother-of-pearl, horn etc, and even marble and onyx. Properly designed pieces in these materials (available in sticks up to three inches (75 mm) or, in some cases, five inches diameter and 58 inches (1500 mm) long) can be very attractive indeed. We should not disdain the use of modern materials – indeed, to do so is one form of snobbery. After all, mahogany was an upstart 'new' material a couple of centuries ago but is now quite venerable! There may come a time when work in modern material is equally sought after.

Finally, work in *metal*. This is not only possible, as I explain in Chapter 8, but can be very effective indeed. The limitation is the lack of rigidity in the O.T. lathe and its accessories, but they can be used if care is taken – and you don't mind brass or steel swarf among the wood shavings! For work in brass, the tools, including those for the cutting frames, have just the right point form and, provided that any serious 'metal shifting' is first done on a normal engineer's lathe, it can, of course, be decorated on the O.T. machine. Let me remind you, too, that many of the 19th century lathe-makers were supplying identical machines to the Royal Ordnance Factory, and these were certainly not occupied in decorating musket butts! Exhibition pieces are frequently displayed in brass, German silver and even stainless steel today, but it must be said that metals producing 'chips' rather than curly swarf are to be preferred.


### Conservation

It is an unfortunate fact that some of the woods we use are now almost endangered species. This is mainly due to their use as veneers – the amount needed for ornamental turning is miniscule by comparison. But, in addition, many of the exotic timber forests are being cut down for other reasons. This means that we should always take care not to waste these exotics and, where possible, build up the sizes we need from smaller pieces. Fortunately, wood turners (of all categories) tend by nature to be people who 'like trees' and there is little risk of the demand from these sources exacerbating the condition of the rain forests.

I have mentioned the problem with ivory already on page 73, and it is very different from those associated with rare woods. Conservation measures taken some years ago pushed up the price of ivory to such an extent that poachers were prepared to take much greater risks than before, and also to go to far greater lengths in obtaining their spoils. Using machine guns from helicopters they have, in some countries, brought the elephant herds almost to extinction, and it is intolerable that turners should contribute to this destruction by buying imported tusks. That is not all. At the conclusion of an International Conference deliberating on the most effective action to take to ensure the survival of these magnificent animals, the United Kingdom, in common with most other countries, has imposed a total ban on the import of raw or worked ivory (there are a very few limited exceptions, such as personal possessions which are antiques) to last for an experimental period of three years. This ban applies even to the tusks of elephants which have died naturally or which have been 'culled' for good reason – there is no means at all of obtaining any imported supplies.

Any ivory already in the possession of turners may still, of course, be used quite legitimately and there is no point at all in not doing so. At present they may also, quite legitimately, sell any supplies or artefacts made from ivory to others *in their own country*. It is advisable that, first, anyone at present holding other than scraps of ivory should take care to preserve the dealer's invoice which should bear the number of the 'licence to import'; or to ensure that they have certified evidence that the piece was imported before July 1975 (this is the date on which rules about the import of ivory were first introduced). If they are in any doubt as to their position they should consult the appropriate Conservation Authority. In the UK this is: The Endangered Species Branch, The Department of the Environment, Room 1105, Tollgate House, Bristol BS8 9DJ. Such consultation is essential if you wish to send a piece you have made to any overseas exhibition, even if it is not for sale.

As I have said, it is quite legitimate to use any pieces of tusk which you already possess, but even here it is clearly necessary to be as economical as possible. Much can be wasted in preparation. Fig. 69 shows the recommended method of preparing a piece when, for example, a box is to be made, and it applies whether you are using the solid or hollow part. At (a) the piece has been sawn off, as near as possible at right angles to the curved centreline; the two cuts are *not* parallel to each other. The shorter length (on the inside of the curve) being no longer than is necessary for its purpose, but bearing in mind

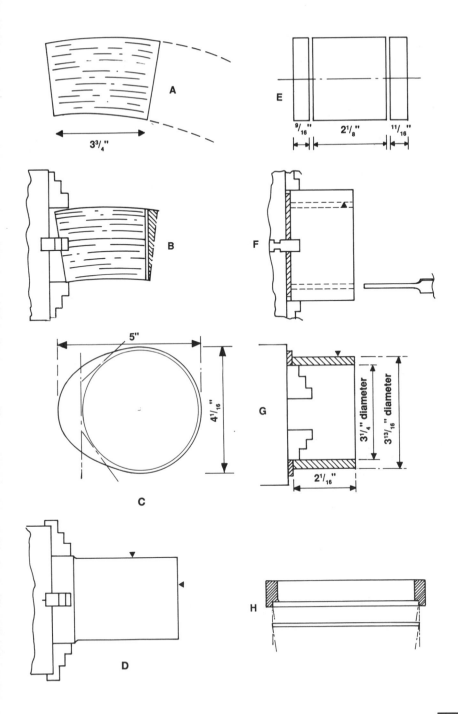

Fig. 69 The method of 'converting' an ivory tusk.

the next step. At (b) one end is being squared off, using as narrow a parting tool as can be handled. The disc is retained for other uses. The other end is then treated likewise. After careful marking out, as at (c), the ovality is reduced by sawing off the surplus. These offcuts may be used for other purposes too, and if of no use to you can be passed over to the lace bobbin fraternity, which will welcome material like this. The alternative is to trepan the oval down to a cylinder, but this may be more wasteful.

The piece is now machined to diameter as at (d), as large as can be managed – I *never* decide on the final size of the box (or whatever) until this stage is reached. You should make sure that the length within the chuck is just enough to make the box lid – or the base if you use that type of construction, (see page 152). These – base and lid – are then parted off as at (e). The solid centre part of the box is then chucked – with a thin packing of wood behind if the four-jaw chuck is being used – and the core trepanned out, leaving a tube of as large an internal diameter as the job in hand allows. (The tool shown in Fig. 61 is used, although it may be necessary to slightly widen the kerf as the tool goes in deeper.) At (g) the bore is being fined out – but I would *not* use a three- or four-jaw chuck for such an operation! The rest of the work on the outside can now be done on a boxwood mandrel.

At (h) I show how the base of such a box can be constructed using one of the slices cut off earlier. The disc is glued to a wooden faceplate and faced both sides, offsetting it to use up the thicker part. It is then machined on the edges to a diameter half way between the ID and the OD of the body of the box, with the edge at a slight angle – say 10 degrees. The bottom of the box is then recessed as shown, also at this angle, and to a diameter such that the smaller diameter of the thin disc will just *not* enter. It can then be sprung into place, with the tapers matching. It should be quite secure, but a spot of glue will make sure. Naturally, there are cases where a thicker base is needed, especially if a decorated lip is needed, but this method has served me well for most cases.

A final point. Even the shavings (both of ivory and wood) should be kept, as they form a very fine polishing medium for those parts of the work on which polishing is permissible and possible.

# 3 PRINCIPLES AND PRACTICE OF SURFACE DECORATION

### Fluting

There is no doubt that fluting is one of the most powerful forms of decoration. It is simple to execute, adds an appearance of strength to slender columns and breaks up what can be an obtrusive solidity to shorter ones. It has its place, too, on the body of plain turned boxes. Selection of the number, spacing and width of the flutes is a matter of personal taste, as well as depending on the nature of the artefact, but Fig. 70 shows three typical samples cut on a practice piece. At (a) we have a series of semicircular flutes cut full depth. They were cut with a narrow tool (No. 95) using the horizontal cutting frame, thus leaving the typical shape at the end of the cut. (The cutter was allowed to run out at the other end.) These could have been cut equally well with the profiled drill, which would leave a semicircular termination at the blank end. On balance, the drill is to be preferred for this type, as it can be run much faster than the HCF (horizontal cutting frame) and so is quicker in execution. (The surface cutting speed is almost irrelevant here, except when working in metal. What matters is the number of individual cuts per inch of length; the higher this figure the better.)

(a)

Fig. 70 (a), (b) and (c). Various types of fluting. ((b) and (c) overleaf.)

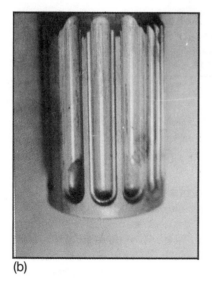
(b)

(c)

At (b) the flutes are wider and deeper, and have a decorative profile. These were cut with the drill, but could have been made with the HCF if a suitable cutter was available. This form of fluting leans towards the opulent and should be used with restraint! In both (a) and (b) the spacing of the flutes can, of course, be varied, and this can have quite an effect on the appearance. In any but the simplest cases, a test piece should be cut to check in the three-dimensional state. Drawings can be deceptive.

At (c) is an example of wide, shallow-cut, fluting, and is cut with the *vertical* cutting frame (VCF). Here the number of flutes governs the depth of cut, which is adjusted so that the original cylindrical surface is only just removed at the apexes of the cuts. The temptation to use a wide cutter to save time should be resisted; a better finish will be obtained with a narrower (not the narrowest!) cutter traversed slowly.

Fig. 71 is an example of *helical fluting* (often misnamed a 'spiral') which is very effective indeed on such items as candle-holder stems. This involves the use of the 'spiral apparatus', which modern turners would call the screw-cutting gears. This is dealt with in another chapter, but we should note that in this case the feedscrew is geared to run *faster* than the mandrel so that the whole must be driven from the mainslide of the sliderest and not from the headstock pulleys. Fluting done with the drill – and this is the recommended method for most cases – presents no problems, but if the universal cutting frame is needed then this must be set at the *lead angle* of the thread or helix, otherwise interference will occur. This is easily calculated as shown in Fig. 72. 'L' is the lead or pitch of the helix. 'C' is the *effective* circumference of the work in way of the flute. This may be taken as PI

Fig. 71 Twisted or helical flutes on a pair of candlesticks.

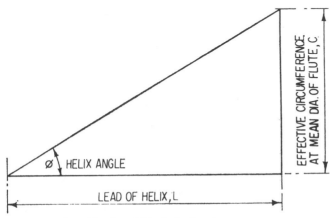

HELIX ANGLE

EFFECTIVE CIRCUMFERENCE
AT MEAN DIA. OF FLUTE, C.

LEAD OF HELIX, L

Fig. 72 The calculation of 'lead angle' for helical work.

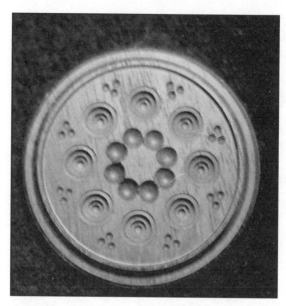

Fig. 73 Simple but effective decoration using the drills.

times the diameter of the column less two thirds of the depth of the flute. Then Tan $\phi = \frac{C}{L}$. Thus for a lead 'L' = 5 inches on an effective diameter of ½-inch, C = 1.571, Tan $\phi$ = 0.314 and $\phi$ = 17.44°. Setting the UCF at 17 degrees is quite near enough – this is by no means critical. Again, the cutting of a short test piece in box or holly is only prudent.

### Beading

This is, in effect, the reverse of fluting. A semicircular bead can be cut (using the HCF) either by using a No. 98, 99 or 107, 108 cutter in one pass, or by machining first one side and then the other using the half-round cutters. The material between beads is then removed using the plain flat-ended cutter. If the drilling instrument is used then the double pass method is essential.

### Bosses and Recesses

These are cut with the drill, or, very occasionally, with the eccentric cutting frame. They can be regarded as a flute or bead of no length, the toolslide being stationary during cutting, and the same techniques are applied, Fig. 73. The one point which *must* be attended to when cutting on the cylinder, is to ensure that the centre of the cutter is exactly at lathe centre height. This consideration applies also to the flute, but the effect of slight off-centre is not anywhere near so evident.

## Circle-based Patterns

Patterns made up of interlaced circles are commonplace – the Olympic Games logo is a case in point. However, when cut either using the eccentric chuck or the eccentric cutting frame (ECF) a whole new dimension is achieved. The specular reflections from the facets of the incisions make even the simplest pattern on the most humdrum of artefacts extremely attractive.

First, a couple of definitions. Fig. 74 shows a circular incision on the end of a circular workpiece of larger diameter. It lies wholly within it, but this need not necessarily be so – in some cases the incised circle can run out from the face on which it is cut. 'O' is the centre of the workpiece, and 'P' that of the incised circle. The distance 'E' is called the **eccentricity** and the half-diameter of the incised circle is called the **radius**. It is important to keep these definitions in mind, as the means of obtaining them can be reversed depending on the method used to achieve the pattern. It will help if you remember that zero radius makes a dot!

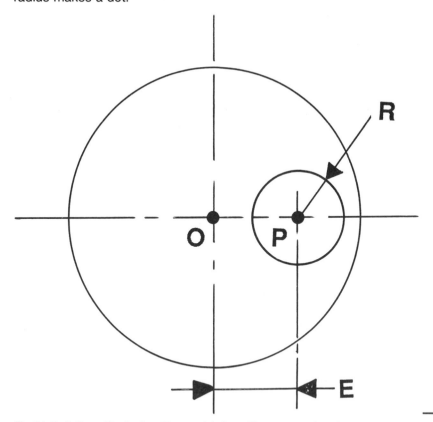

Fig. 74 Definition of 'radius' and 'eccentricity' used in ornamental turning.

Fig. 75 is taken from Holtzapffel's book on ornamental turning (Vol. V, Plate IX). The white lines indicate the track of the extreme point of the tool; in reality the black spaces between will be formed of highly reflective facets (provided that your tools are properly sharpened!) so that diagrams give no idea of the final appearance.

In the top row, the eccentricity is equal to the radius, so that every cut passes through the centre of the workpiece. That in the centre of the top row comprises 32 cuts (indexed at every third division of the 96-hole plate) and if cut deep enough so that no flat surface remains, presents a very attractive effect indeed. However, if we *omit* some of the cuts we get, on the left, a 'tartan' pattern (indexed on the 96 ring at 2-10-11-12-13-14-15-16, and then 18-26-28-29-30-31-32, and so on) which will have some flat surfaces showing between the wider spaced incisions. The 'Floral' pattern on the right hand side is indexed, again on the 96 circle, every other hole, with a gap of FOUR holes at every fifth circle cut.

The second row shows the effect if the radius is *less* than the eccentricity. The circular incisions lie in a ring around the plain centre of the workpiece. (Although, of course, there is no reason why a further series of decorations should not be applied there as well.) Again, the centre example uses 48 cuts, every two on the 96 hole plate. That on the left is similar to the tartan above, but as you can see, it comprises five cuts close together (adjacent holes in the 96 ring) with two cuts in between spaced four holes apart, six groups of circles altogether. That on the right is similar, but has eight groups, with corresponding changes in the spacing. In the third row the radius is *greater* than the eccentricity. Similar effects are obtained to the previous ones, but the angle of intersection of the cuts is greater.

Even more interesting variations can be observed if a complete section of the pattern is omitted, and you may find one of these in some of the examples given later in the book. The importance of experimenting cannot be over-emphasised, for to continue to use 'classic' arrangements such as these can become tedious. In addition, practice in manipulation, checking the effect of different relative depths of cut, and changing the proportions between radius and eccentricity, is all of the greatest value – besides being great fun!

### The Barleycorn

The example in the centre of the second row, where radius is less than eccentricity, can be manipulated in a special way to form one of the most attractive patterns of all. This requires the basic incisions just to touch each other, and Fig. 76 shows the principle. At 'a' we have a set of circular cuts – there might be twelve, say, to complete the ring,

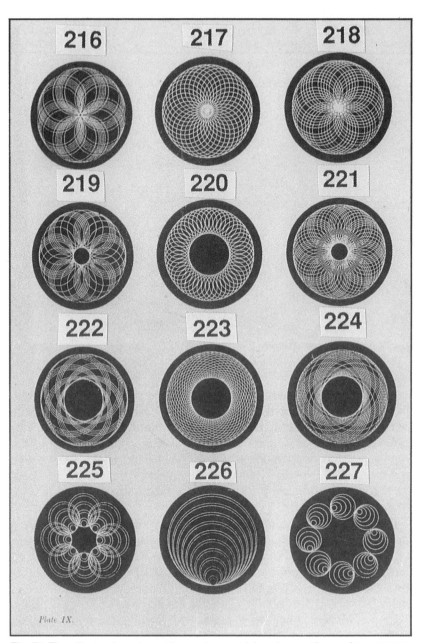

Fig. 75 The effects of varying radius and eccentricity when cutting surface patterns. (*Holtz V*)

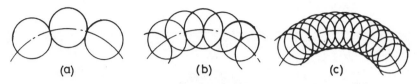

DEVELOPMENT OF THE 'BARLEYCORN'

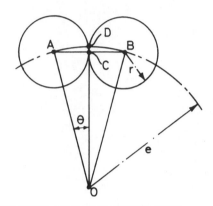

GEOMETRY OF BASIC CIRCLE RING

Fig. 76 The 'barleycorn' pattern.

just touching. At 'b' a second set has been cut in between the first set. Then at 'c' two more series have been cut between those at 'b'. If there were twelve circles at 'a' this would form a 'barleycorn of 4 × 12'. This can vary enormously, depending on the size of the piece and the intensity of the decoration required; I have used up to 40 × 8 and down to 8 × 3. However, whatever the proportions the depth of cut *must* always be sufficient to bring the peaks between the cuts to a sharp point.

The condition for touching circles is shown at 'd' in Fig. 76. OA is the eccentricity, and BC is the radius (marked 'e' and 'r'). Look at this carefully. The circles touch at the point 'C' *NOT AT 'D'*. So, for 12 circles (say) 'r' will *not* be one twenty-fourth of the circumference of the base circle, $2\pi \times OA$, but half the length of the chord AB. This can easily be worked out; e.g. for 12 circles the angle $\phi$ will be 15 degrees. AC = r = eSIN $\theta$. However, it is easier to use a 'circle spacing table'. That given below is taken from *The Model Engineer's Handbook* (Argus Books) and will serve for most conditions. There is no need to work to the precision implied by the number of decimal places, though! In all ornamental work it is essential to make trial cuts before starting.

## CIRCLE SPACING TABLE

To set out a number of circles 'N' of diameter 'd' (= 2r) which just touch each other on a pitch circle diameter 'D' (= 2e) the following may be used, where $c = \frac{d}{D}$. The general rule is that $c = \text{SIN}(180/N)$.

| N | c | N | c | N | c | N | c |
|---|---|---|---|---|---|---|---|
| 3 | 0.8660 | 15 | 0.2079 | 27 | 0.11609 | 39 | 0.08046 |
| 4 | 0.7071 | 16 | 0.1951 | 28 | 0.11197 | 40 | 0.07846 |
| 5 | 0.5878 | 17 | 0.1837 | 29 | 0.10812 | 41 | 0.07654 |
| 6 | 0.5000 | 18 | 0.1736 | 30 | 0.10453 | 42 | 0.07473 |
| 7 | 0.4339 | 19 | 0.1646 | 31 | 0.10117 | 43 | 0.07299 |
| 8 | 0.3827 | 20 | 0.1564 | 32 | 0.09801 | 44 | 0.07133 |
| 9 | 0.3420 | 21 | 0.1490 | 33 | 0.09505 | 45 | 0.06975 |
| 10 | 0.3090 | 22 | 0.1423 | 34 | 0.09226 | 46 | 0.06824 |
| 11 | 0.2817 | 23 | 0.1362 | 35 | 0.08964 | 47 | 0.06679 |
| 12 | 0.2588 | 24 | 0.1305 | 36 | 0.08715 | 48 | 0.06540 |
| 13 | 0.2393 | 25 | 0.1253 | 37 | 0.08480 | 49 | 0.06407 |
| 14 | 0.0225 | 26 | 0.1205 | 38 | 0.08258 | 50 | 0.06275 |
| 60 | 0.0523 | 120 | 0.0262 | 180 | 0.01745 | 360 | 0.00873 |

This table does not include some ratios which (given the ornamental turners' preoccupation with factors of 12) are often used. For the record, these are added below.

| N | 56 | 72 | 96 | 144 | 192 | 360 |
|---|---|---|---|---|---|---|
| c | 0.056 | 0.044 | 0.033 | 0.022 | 0.016 | 0.009 |

Before leaving this pattern I must refer to an interesting variation – the **double barleycorn**. Having cut one, say 4 × 48, a second barleycorn of 8 × 24 can be cut on top of it. The radius of this second pattern will be very slightly smaller than twice the radius for the first pattern, and the exact setting must be found by trial – not difficult, as the tool point must drop into the vee of the first series of cuts at the meeting points. The depths of cut must be exactly the same for both sets. It is well worth a trial. (It can be seen in the outer ring of Fig. 30, p. 37)

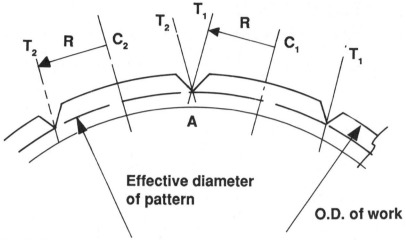

Fig. 77 The barleycorn on the cylinder, C-C, Centre of ECF; R, radius of ECF; T-T, track of cutter; A, incision widened after two passes.

### The Barleycorn on the Cylinder

The Barleycorn cut on the cylinder is a very attractive decoration indeed, especially if it is cut fairly deeply. The procedure is exactly as before, but there is a problem, explained in Fig. 77. The roots of the incisions now lie below the surface, and at an effective diameter which is less than the O.D. of the workpiece and not easy to calculate. (Another difference – it is no problem – is that the angle of the incised grooves will be greater than that of the cutter, as the latter meets the surface on a curve.)

In determining the radius to set on the ECF, start by deducting an amount equal to half the estimated *width* of the cut from the O.D. of the workpiece, and use this as the effective diameter when using the table. Set the ECF very slightly less than this. Now make trial cuts on two circles indexed to the base number of the pattern, (e.g. for a 3 × 16 index at every 6th hole on the 96 plate). Deepen the cut a little at a time until you see that the roots of the cut are just meeting. Now check the crests. If these form a sharp point, well and good; if not, very slightly reduce the setting on the ECF and try again. Repeat this until you get an exact match at the root coupled with a sharp crest. It is, of course, best to check this setting on a test piece first, but as each deeper cut erases the effects of previous ones the pattern will not be spoiled by the trial cuts – unless, of course, you are a long way out in your initial estimate. There is, incidentally, no harm done if the barleycorn crests lie a little below the normal surface of the cylinder, and in some eyes this is an advantage. The barleycorn can, of course, be cut on the slant on a surface, and on slight tapers on the cylinder.

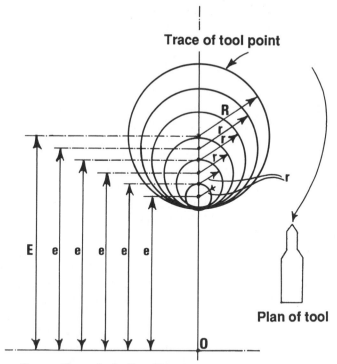

**Trace of tool point**

**Plan of tool**

**Formation of shell pattern**
**O = axis of headstock mandrel**
**R = initial radius of cutter circle**
**r = subsequent cutter circles**
**E = initial sliderest setting**
**e = subsequent sliderest setting**

Fig. 78 The 'shell' pattern. A variation is found in Fig. 130.

### Linear Groupings of Circles

A 'straight line' barleycorn can, of course, be cut – around the body of a square box, for example – but unless it runs out completely the end circles will not form complete 'corns'. If such a pattern is required – to decorate a square column, for example – then the final circles at each end must be reduced in radius progressively, the final one ending as a dot. No rules can be given for these settings, and a test piece must be cut first.

The most attractive of the linear spacings is the **shell pattern**. Examples will be found later in the book and in the fourth row of Fig. 75. Fig. 78 shows the arrangement and sequence of cutting. Remembering that the lines represent the roots of the incisions and that the cuts are deep enough to form pointed crests, the resemblance to a cockleshell is obvious. To cut a ring of shells, the mandrel is held using the index in any convenient dividing ring. The sliderest is offset by the initial eccentricity 'E' and the ECF set to initial radius 'R'. All the largest circles are then cut, one after the other, estimating the required depth at this stage. The ECF radius is then reduced (for the six-line pattern shown) to ⅚ of the original, and the sliderest eccentricity reduced by the same amount. The depth of cut should be enough to make a sharp crest, but if not, the first set of circles is recut before proceeding with the second set. The depth screw is then locked. The ECF radius and the sliderest eccentricity are then reduced by the amounts used before and the process repeated until the final cut – a small cone – is made. A careful check is made throughout to ensure that *all* the circles coincide at the base or root of the shell.

Most of those seen in later examples have been cut with the vee-pointed tool (80 to 100 degrees included angle) but an alternative is to use the half-vee, making incisions which are vertical on the outer circumference. This can, in some circumstances, produce a more striking pattern. A further alternative is to cut *pairs* of incisions close together, with wider spacing between each pair, Fig. 79. And although Fig. 78 suggests a ring of shells on the workpiece a single pattern of large diameter with a multitude of incisions is very effective in breaking up the large plain surface of a box lid.

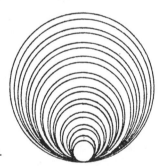

Fig. 79 The double-cut shell pattern.

### Combinations of Patterns

The total decoration of larger surfaces is effected by the judicious combination of a number of diverse patterns. Fig. 80 shows one such, with a modified tartan surrounded by a ring of barleycorns, which is in turn enclosed by a compound pattern of large and small shells. The photograph cannot do justice to the effect, but it does show up one defect which afflicts anyone using a slice from a large tusk – the presence of the 'nerve' or core near the centre. This is almost always present in the larger section, and since making this piece I have adopted the practice of trepanning out the core and letting in a smaller

Fig. 80 A large compound pattern three inches diameter. This could be cut with either the eccentric chuck or the cutting frame, but would take a very long time with the former. (The photograph does not do justice to the sharpness of the incisions.)

disc (coinciding with the outline of the centre pattern) taken from the smaller end of the tooth.

In the design of all patterns, especially compound ones, the use of the tympan chuck (see page 124 helps a great deal. The individual patterns can be drawn on paper and superimposed to judge the effect and, after adjustment, a sector of the pattern drawn in full (or even the complete design) before any cutting is done.

### Elliptical Patterns

Almost all of those described can also be described as ellipses, and the super-imposition of series of ellipses at different angles can be very effective indeed. The elliptical barleycorn is attractive, but does need more than ordinary care if the *basis* also is elliptical – the 'equal division of the ellipse' apparatus (page 132) is needed, and even with this some adjustment from place to place is usually necessary.

It may be apposite at this stage to remark that all the patterns so far described can be cut using either the eccentric cutting frame *or* the eccentric chuck. If the chuck is used, then the *eccentricity* is obtained by offsetting the chuck and the *radius* by adjusting the sliderest. If the ECF is used (the work being mounted on a plain chuck or faceplate) then *eccentricity* is obtained by movement of the sliderest and *radius* by adjustment of the slide of the cutting frame. Indexing is done by the tangent screw of the chuck, if used, but with the ECF the mandrel is indexed on the pulley dividing circles.

### Depths of Cut

In general, deep cutting results in more specular reflections from the facets, and this tends to mean coarse spacing. Fine spacing of the cuts imposes shallow depths (if deep cutting is done with a fine spacing the whole pattern will be recessed below the surface) and although the effect is still very attractive the sparkling reflections are often dimmed. If wide spacing is used with relatively shallow cuts then there must remain some flat plateau between the incisions. This applies especially to the tartan and similar patterns. In ivory and some of the woods these flats can be polished before cutting the incisions, but seldom achieve the reflective properties of the pattern furrows, due to the different cutting action of the cutting frame tools and facing tools traversed on the sliderest.

With most woods, many practitioners accept this situation by deliberately 'matting' the surface before cutting the pattern, and this matting considerably enhances the contrast. This is effected by *graining*. After facing the workpiece, a series of close-pitched concentric grooves is cut on the face. A *very* sharp vee-pointed tool is used, the angle being from 100 to 120 degrees inclusive. The cuts are spaced at from 0.015 to 0.025 inches, and the depth only just sufficient to form sharp crests. Typically 0.006 to 0.008 inches. This is very effective, but it does have a disadvantage; over the years the 'grains' collect dust, and can be very difficult to clean!

### Basket or Wickerwork

The surface patterns so far are (except for the barleycorn) appropriate only to flat or slightly conical surfaces. Decoration of the cylinder is equally important, and basketwork of various types forms the basis. Fig. 81 shows a variety of examples, taken from Vol. V of Holtzapffel's *Turning and Mechanical Manipulation* of 1884. The specimens are all about 1½ inch diameter and all are to the same scale.

The geometry of the true basket, top left, is shown in Fig. 82. The vertical cutting frame is used, with a flat-ended cutterbit, the projection of which is adjusted to obtain the desired length and depth of segment or 'scallop'. (In Fig. 81 the tool was 0.05 inch wide.) Taking top left as an example, with twelve segments to the circle an initial cut is made, not too deep, after which the work is indexed eight holes on the 96 plate and another cut made. These two are deepened until the crest between them becomes a sharp edge, when the depth stop is locked.

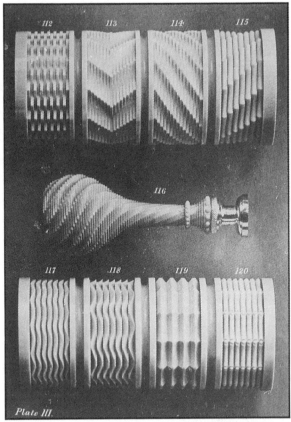

Fig. 81 Examples of different forms of basketwork. The columns are about 1½ inches diameter and the seal is to the same scale. (*Holtz V*)

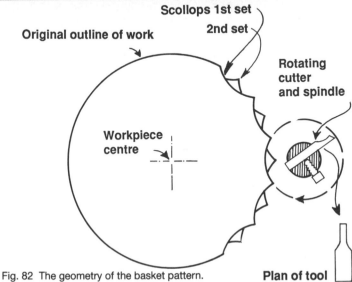

Fig. 82 The geometry of the basket pattern.

The cuts are then made right round the work at index 8-16-24-32 etc. The sliderest is then traversed by the width of the tool – very slightly less if absolute exactitude is not possible – and the process repeated but this time at index 4-12-20-28 etc. – and so on, alternating between the two index series until the pattern is complete. As a matter of artistic principle there should always be an odd number of rows, so that first and last are in line.

The method for the *helical* wickerwork is similar, except that this time each row of cuts is moved one index division forwards, say 8-16-24-32 etc followed by 9-17-25-33 etc. A little care over the design of this one is needed, to ensure that the width of the cuts and the number around the circumference is such that the final cuts align with the first. The chevron form is exactly the same except that the order of indexing is reversed on reaching the centre cut. An odd number of rows is needed here, too. The right hand style in the top row – like a bamboo basket – is obtained simply by using a semi-circular cutter No. 99.

The patterns on the lower row may need a little explanation. Cutting procedure is to cut adjacent rows with a left pointed quarter round tool No. 97 throughout, traversing the cutter width between each. Then change to the RH tool, No. 96 and recut all, but indexed at the intermediate holes. A sharper pattern is obtained, as seen, if the half angle tools, Nos. 93 and 92, are used. A little study of Fig. 81 will reveal the method for the others, but the last, bottom RH, has been further embellished by applying a bead cutting drill at the apex of the union between adjacent segments.

The seal handle seen in Fig. 81 shows a fine example of this type of decoration. In the event the 'curvelinear' apparatus was used, but this is not essential. All rows have an identical number of segments, and all rows are the same width. The differential indexing between rows is identical, too. The difference is that for each row the depth stop on the tool carrier must be readjusted to bring the apex between segments just at, or very slightly below, the profile – which can, of course, be hand turned in the absence of a copying attachment.

### Diamond Pattern

Fig. 83 shows an ebony box with a diamond pattern on the cylinder. This is no more than the 'twist' already considered for decorating columns, but with a second series reversed – the reversal effected by setting an additional idler wheel in the gear train of the spiral apparatus. It is, however, desirable that the ends of the incisions of opposite hand should meet where they run out. Easy enough to achieve this at one end, but some figuring is needed to persuade them to meet at

Fig. 83 The 'diamond' pattern on an ebony box. The lid is decorated with one of the patterns shown in Fig. 75.

both ends. The rule is simple. The height of the decoration, H, must be a whole number times the Lead of the helix, L, divided by the number of incisions N which run round the circumference, i.e. $H = y\frac{L}{N}$, y being a whole number. If you want the diamonds to contain a specific angle, then the rule is that $H = y\text{TAN } \frac{1}{2}\phi \times \frac{\pi D}{N}$, where $\phi$ is the included angle at the top of the diamond. There are some constraints, of course. The exact lead available is limited by the size of the change wheels available and, of course, the diameter of the box has to fit the available material.

### The Fish Pattern

This is one of the classical patterns, and its successful execution is generally taken to mark the transition from beginner to improver in O.T.

circles! Fig. 84 shows the first as cut by Holtzapffel, (see also Fig. 131 on page 153). Elaborate though it may seem, the whole is formed of interlacing circular cuts with a 45 degree half angle tool. It is testing, both because the settings must be made very accurately if the effect is to be obtained, and because it involves some very deep cutting indeed. Fig 85a shows the nature of the problem. The cutter is a No. 93 at 45 degrees, used in the EFC at an angle of 12 degrees to the

Fig. 84 The fish pattern, as cut by John Jacob Holtzapffel II, on a piece of highly figured ivory. (*Holtz V*)

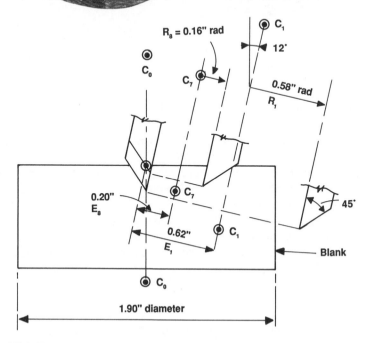

Fig. 85(a) Showing the very deep cutting involved in making the 'fish'.

mandrel axis. It will be seen that the initial cuts, (marked as $R_1$) could be very deep indeed. Fig. 85b emphasises the point. This is a cross section (not to scale) at about the centre of the fish body. We can reduce the cutter load to some extent by pre-forming the blank, as shown in Fig. 85c. The chucking piece can be longer with advantage – it is *imperative* that there be not the slightest slip during cutting. The OD of two inches allows for slight reduction after the pattern is cut to refine the proportions. It is also necessary to see that the height is not less than the ¾ inch shown, both to avoid interference between tool and chuck, and to allow for subsequent parting off. The pattern is, of course, cut on a separate piece of ivory and let into the main body of the lid later.

It is evident that the cutter may be cutting on the sides as well as on the slant end, so that sharpening must be carried out on the two sides, ac and bd, as well as on the end, ab. This sharpening must be meticulously carried out as previously described. There will be no opportunity of resharpening once cutting has started. A trial piece should be cut, perhaps to form just one 'fish', using either African blackwood or box, to get used to the deep cutting and to ascertain the best cutting speed. There is considerable shock loading on the ECF. (I used around 900 rpm.) I also recommend that you do not start until you know that you will have NO interruptions until the whole job is finished; and that you prepare a worksheet showing all the settings, and cross them off as you complete each!

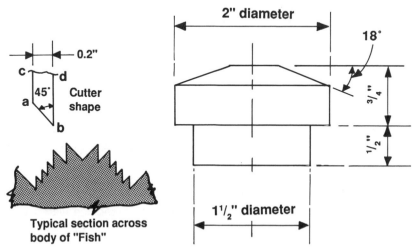

Fig. 85(b) A cross section of the fish body.

Fig. 85(c) Suggested shape of the blank.

I have deliberately given no 'chapter and verse' descriptions of the making of previous patterns as there is no substitute for personal trials and experience – and it is much more fun to work it out for yourself than to be told exactly how to do it. However, the fish *is* rather complex, and even if you can obtain a copy of Holtzapffel Volume V (and can afford it) the description therein is confusing to those not accustomed to this type of manipulation. So, I hope that the following will help.

After chucking the blank is formed as in Fig. 85c, and if any time elapses between this step and the remainder it should be refaced. The 144 row dividing circle will be used throughout, and the index should be checked for secure engagement; the interrupted cuts might be severe enough to dislodge it unless it is secure. Proceed as follows.

(1) Set the sliderest across the bed at 12 degrees and the ECF to zero. Adjust the sliderest so that the ECF forms an exact point in the centre of the workpiece. This may mean adjusting the height of the sliderest. Set the S/R index to zero, and check the reading on the ECF feedscrew index – it may not centre at the zero mark on its index. Allow for this in what follows.

(2) Set the radius of the ECF to 0.58 and the S/R (sliderest) to 0.62 ins eccentricity from the work centre, and the mandrel index at zero (144).

(3) Running at about 900 rpm, very carefully advance the cutter until the depth of cut at the centre of the block is 0.2 ins. Lock the depth stop.

(4) Repeat this process with the mandrel index at 36, 72, and 108, Fig. 86a.

(5) *Reduce* the ECF radius by 0.06 ins; *reduce* the eccentricity of the S/R by the same 0.06 ins and adjust the depth stop to *reduce* the depth of cut by 0.02 ins. Make a set of four cuts at each of the previous index settings – Fig. 86b.

(6) Repeat the procedure of step (5) above, reducing the three settings each time, until you have made (in all) eight cuts at each of four index settings. The result should be as in Fig. 86c, and the final settings should be R = 0.16, E = 0.20 and depth 0.06 ins.

(7) The next step is to cut away all the unwanted 'scales' in the shaded area of Fig. 86d.

(8) Traverse the sliderest so that the ECF is clear of the work and chuck. *Either* remove the tool, stone a flat about 0.01 inch wide on the point and relap the cutting edges, *or* replace with a tool of this shape previously prepared, taking care to get the same projection.

(9) Adjust the ECF to a radius of about 0.33 inches, and check that the rotating tool will clear the workpiece.

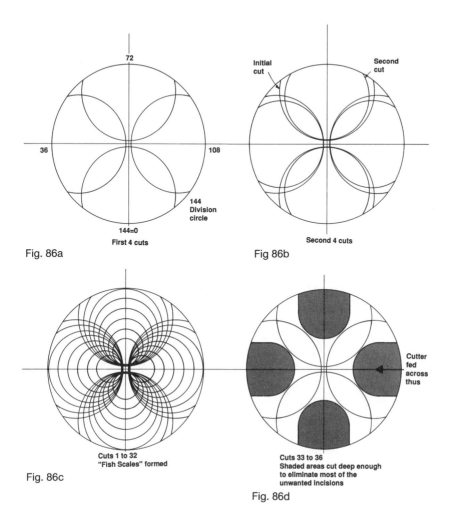

Fig. 86a

72

36                     108

144
Division
circle

144=0
First 4 cuts

Fig 86b

Initial
cut

Second
cut

Second 4 cuts

Fig. 86c

Cuts 1 to 32
"Fish Scales" formed

Fig. 86d

Cutter
fed
across
thus

Cuts 33 to 36
Shaded areas cut deep enough
to eliminate most of the
unwanted incisions

Fig. 86 First sequence of operations used when cutting the fish pattern.

(10) With mandrel index at zero (144) very carefully traverse the S/R inwards to remove the scales over the plateau, going only far enough to leave a *small* ridge along the sides of the two fishes. If necessary repeat this with slightly greater radius and depth. Then *lock* both the depth stop and the fluting stop on the sliderest.

(11) Repeat this process against the locked stops at index settings 36, 72 and 108 – Fig. 86d.

(12) We now form the fishes' tails. Traverse well away from the work. Reset ECF to 0.18 radius, and the depth stop to about 0.03 inch *deeper* than before. With division index at **13** and **23** make trial

cuts to form the two sides of the tail – Fig. 87. If necessary adjust the radius slightly to get the best effect – perhaps as far as 0.2 in. When satisfied with the appearance *lock up* both depth and fluting stops at this setting.

(13) Repeat this process at index settings of 49 & 59, 85 & 95, and 121 & 131. Inspect to see if any further adjustments might improve the shape and repeat if need be.

(14) At the *same* settings of ECF and S/R form the 'scallops' around the rim of the pattern at index settings of 4-32-40-68-76-104-112-140, missing those already cut (Fig. 87.)

(15) Take a skim off the OD to bring both tails and scallops to exactly, or very slightly less than, a semi-circle. Check all work, and then part off to the thickness required.

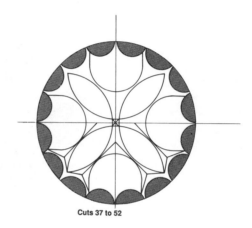

Cuts 37 to 52

Fig. 87 Shaded areas form the fishes 'tails' and also remove remaining incisions.

You may be concerned to notice that there seems to be an uncut projection on the back of each fish. This is as it should be – the creature's dorsal fin!

The pattern can be formed with three fishes, or even with six, but I leave you to work out the settings for yourself! Make trials with boxwood first, of course, but don't be alarmed if the deep cutting leaves the edges of the scales slightly rough.

This chapter cannot possibly cover all the variations in ornamentation – a number of 18th and 19th century authors have written whole books on this aspect alone. I am conscious, too, that I have not really done justice to the use of the 'drilling instrument' – almost lace-like decoration can be achieved just by drilling judiciously spaced holes!

But those I have described can form a solid basis for further experiment and development, especially of patterns in combination, and to go further would only deprive you of the fun and sense of achievement in working them out for yourself! I will end by commending to you the distinction between 'technical expertise' and 'artistic merit'. The two do not necessarily go together and a judicious blending of simple patterns will often attract more approbation than an elaborate piece which has been embellished with examples of the use of every available accessory in the practitioner's cupboard! See Fig. 9 page 18 as an example!

# 4 SETTING UP THE MACHINE

You must start by realising that, whether the machine be a Holtzapffel, Evans, Fenn or any other, it is likely to be perhaps 100 years old. (Holtz. No. 2456 was made in 1890; the last made was No. 2549.) And quite a number may be much older; my Holtz No. 484 was made in 1805. This fact is relevant in several ways. Firstly, although these machines were made by first-class craftsmen, under very rigorous supervision, they did not have the benefit of even the most elementary modern aids to production. Few would have had a micrometer, for example, and the dial indicator was unknown. The user of any lathe of this period was expected to spend some time in setting up before using, and to take precautions against inaccuracy. (The sliderest of my No. 484 was made entirely by filing and scraping.)

Secondly, there will inevitably be some wear – not so much in the headstock bearings as these were usually hard steel running in hard steel bushes (or case-hardened wrought iron), but often on the slides. In some cases this wear may be slight but be in a position where serious consequences result. A third, associated, problem is that over these long periods the castings can suffer dimensional change, again putting things out of line.

This means that you must start by checking over the whole of the machine before using it for the first time. In addition, I recheck mine every year or so; relatively easy once the machine has been set right in the first place. But this is due to a fourth feature of these old machines; they are torsionally very flimsy even though the frame may appear to be extremely stiff. This is the first thing to check. For this, you need a really good quality spirit level and, in using it, to remember that all spirit levels are calibrated when bearing full length. So, when checking *across* the bed you must set it on a parallel of sufficient length. With this, set the iron bed level both longitudinally and across the bed at both ends. You may well be surprised to find how unlevel your floor is! Fit carefully-made hardwood (I use lignum) packing under each corner of the supporting frame. If you are going to screw the machine down, then check the levels again after tightening the screws.

Now slacken the screws or nuts which secure the metal bearers to the frame, to allow them to find a natural position, and then re-tighten. Repeat the previous check. You can now be fairly sure that the bearers are both level and free from any strain trying to twist them. I usually check the guide surface for straightness, too, but this does need special equipment and, in any case, serious error here would require considerable work to correct. But it *is* worth checking the width of the space between the front and rear shears, and is easily done with a test block slightly smaller than the space and a set of feeler gauges. You can then identify any spots where there is an error, and avoid these if possible. This also reveals a much more common, and inherently troublesome, fault: that of burrs on the guide face, which must be removed with a fine file.

### *Headstock*

Bearing wear is, as I have said, usually slight. With the common mandrel headstock it is possible to correct any slight wear by lapping the front, conical bearing with metal polish, and tightening up the rear thrust cone. If the latter is at all ridged, then it will pay to have the cone professionally reground, specifying that the cone must be true to the body. Treating the conical socket in the mandrel is another matter. I know of one which has been recut, using standard slocumbe centre drills, very low speed, and extreme pressure; after using up four such drills a perfect seating was obtained! But the one thing that matters is that the point of the adjusting screw should be co-axial with the nominal line of the headstock. If it is not, the alignment of the mandrel will change every time an adjustment is made. If the cone and socket are 'not too bad' the best thing to do is merely to hone off the worst of the ridges and leave it be.

With the traversing mandrel type of bearing there is nothing to be done. Some of the later lathes had separate hard steel bushes, and in this case new ones can be made of bronze. Wear is usually on the lower quadrant of the bearing, due to the belt tension down to the treadle. Fig. 88 shows the difference between the modern motor/ countershaft drive and the old treadle; both belts are in place in the photo. (Treadle drive is still best for some operations – screwcutting with the traversing mandrel especially.) Frankly, unless the bearings are in really bad shape it is best to leave them until you meet trouble arising from this cause.

This assured, the next step is to align the headstock. This is imperative. Although the machine is not a sliding lathe, mandrel misalignment will cause trouble. Fortunately the job is not too difficult. Chuck a piece of lignum or boxwood which will turn to about 1½ inch diameter or as large as your chuck will hold, and four to six inches long. Rough turn it, and then turn a couple of bobbins, one near the chuck and one remote, as shown in my sketch, Fig. 89. Use your

Fig. 88 A countershaft drive. The drive pulley is made from laminated sheets of mahogany (Fenn) glued to a metal bush with Araldite.

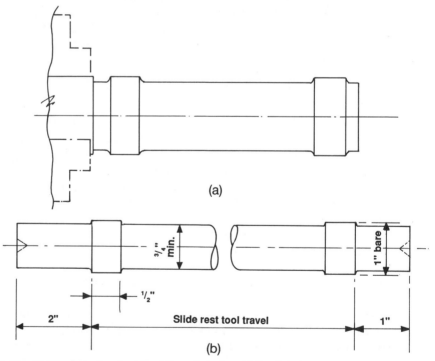

(a)

(b)

Fig. 89 Mandrels for checking lathe alignment. (a) For headstock alignment; (b) for sliderest, between centres. They can be made of hard wood.

micrometer to make these bobbins exactly the same diameter. Set up your scribing block, with a dial indicator if at all possible, but working with feeler gauges if you have none. Check the attitude of the test piece by running across the bobbins with the index set in the 96, 24, 48 and 72 holes of the dividing circle, noting down the readings on each bobbin at each setting. Take the mean of the four readings and compare them. Repeat the exercise with the scribing block again to take the same measurements, but this time with the gauge or feelers acting in front of the test bar, the block engaging with the inner edge of the front shear of the bed. The first set of readings will show whether or not the headstock mandrel is tilted in the vertical plane, the second will show whether it aligns with the centreline of the bed. Any errors should be corrected with shims until the difference is less than 0.001 inch in four inches. Bring it down less if you can!

You now know that the mandrel of the lathe is as near parallel to the axis of the bed as can be achieved. Once done, this should 'stay put' for many years, and you can fix the shims in place with Araldite or similar.

*Tailstock*

The tailstock poppet also must align in the same way. A rough check can be made by bringing the cone centre close to a centre in the headstock and examining them under a glass. This will reveal any gross error. The check must be done with the poppet full out and full back. Any difference in the two positions means that the tailstock is slantendicular across the bed or (less likely) in the vertical plane. Again, correct with shims. To make a final test, set a small piece of box or holly in the chuck, face it truly, with no 'pip'. Bring up the tailstock and gently impact the centre to the face; then rotate the mandrel. If all is well you will get a dot, but any misalignment will draw a tiny circle. Further adjustment should be made to eliminate this. However, you may well find, as I did, that the tailstock is already 'high' compared with the headstock, in which case you must set further parallel shims under the latter. Once these checks have been carried out you have a machine which is, within the limits imposed by errors on the bed, capable of turning parallel. However, please note that *any* change under the footings of the lathe – movement of the floor, or even the presence of a very heavy visitor – can change this condition. Fortunately any such change is usually either too slight to be troublesome or so great as to be evident immediately.

*Sliderest*

There will almost certainly be trouble here due to wear – not so much in the slides as on the bottom surface of the banjo which sits on the bed. This *must* be corrected, see Fig. 90. If the sliderest (or the tool holder) does not lie parallel to the bed longitudinally, there will be a mismatch when using the vertical cutting frame to cut (e.g) a basket-work pattern, as shown at (a). Then, if it does not lie truly when set across the bed, any tool in the eccentric cutting frame will cut deeper at top or bottom, as in (b).

The initial check is to set the slide parallel to the bed as near as possible and use your scribing block to check that the top face lies parallel. Correct this by setting shim under one side or other of the banjo support. This is likely to need alteration, so do not fix it permanently. To check the lateral alignment you can either use the same method, but with the slide across the bed; or face a piece of wood on the faceplate, as large a diameter as possible, and then traverse a sharp tool right across with the mandrel locked. A check with the scribing block (or, of course, a vernier height gauge if your workshop runs to one!) will show up any misalignment crossways. Correct this with shims. You will almost certainly have to go through this procedure two or three times, as each affects the other. Once done, however, you can make a permanent correction by filing or scraping the underside of the banjo, or by fixing the shims with

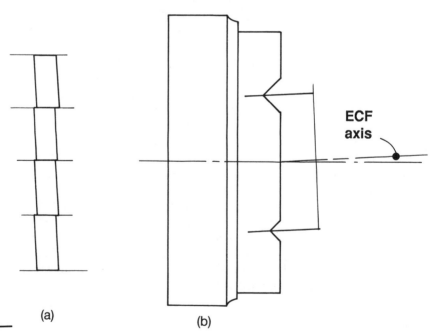

(a)   (b)

110

Fig. 90 Effects of sliderest misalignment (a) on a basket pattern and (b) with the ECF.

Fig. 91 Alignment and gib adjusting screws. The latter may be rather brittle.

Araldite. The shim can be stuck to the underside of the banjo cradle if you like. My own machine has had such shims under the sliderest for about ten years now, just waiting for me to have time to get busy with a scraper!

I should, of course, have warned you first to correct all slop in the slide gibs and especially to see that there is no dirt or burrs affecting the movement. In this connection an *essential* tool for those owning ornamental lathes is a screwdriver with a fairly wide blade the thickness of which has been made to fit the heads of the sliderest screws *exactly*. Two such are seen in Fig. 91. These screws can be very stubborn on an old machine, and they are also prone to brittleness. So, if they are stiff use plenty of release oil (or a mixture of 'Oil of Wintergreen' and diesel oil) left to soak overnight. I had to leave one soaking for two days and even then it needed the topslide heating in boiling water before the screw would move. You will, of course, be aware of the trick of applying a torque to *tighten* the screw first, and while under such torque, giving the screwdriver a tap on the end with a hammer!

The next step is to check that the bottom of the toolholder (receptacle, to give it its traditional name) also lies parallel to the top of the bed. This can be found to be very scarred. Clean it up with a file or, better still, a milling cutter after having checked how much must come off; it will almost certainly be a taper cut and may taper from side to side. Lack of alignment here, either way, can cause the same troubles shown in Fig. 90. I have said nothing about the vee-slides to the topslide. These will, of course, be worn, and may be contributing to the faults we have just corrected. However, my experience is that unless you are prepared to carry out a major re-machining job on the rest, and make new slides, it is best to leave well alone here after removing any burrs and ridges.

The sliderest is now in a healthy condition, and can be set up. Start by setting the elevating screw at about mid travel and adjust the thickness of the steel plate which lies in the bottom of the toolholder so that the top of a standard (and, if possible, unused) tool lies exactly at centre height. Make a new steel packing if the tool point is very far out. Now set a test mandrel between centres, similar to Fig. 89, but long enough to cover the full travel of the main slide. Turn a bobbin at each end, and adjust the stop screw (seen just below the fluting stop in Fig. 91) until both bobbins are the same size. The rest is now turning parallel and the screw can be locked. Turn the rest sideways, and machine the face of a test piece, as large as you can manage. Adjust the other stop until this face is either dead flat or very slightly concave. *It must on no account be convex.* I recommend that you carry out each of these checks three times, to assure 'repeatability'; if they don't work out very nearly the same for each trial, something is loose and you must seek out and correct the fault. But watch out for the odd bit of wood shaving getting between the adjusting screw and the stop-peg! You can now make the final check on the alignment of the rest itself. First, set a vertical cutting frame (or the universal set in the vertical mode) and make three cuts, one above the other, using a tool about 0.1 inch wide. They should lie dead in line, and not as in Fig. 90a. Next, offer your eccentric cutting frame to the machined face you tested earlier. Check with a blunt tool and feelers that there is the same gap between tool and workpiece – using the maximum radius of the cutter – at the four dead centres. You will not achieve perfection unless you are fortunate, but anything more than about 0.001 inch should be looked at.

### A Final Check

The final test has nothing whatever to do with setting up the machine, but I would like you to carry it out just the same! Set a test piece between centres; your previous one will do if you turn off the bobbins. Machine it parallel. Now take another cut, traversing carefully but using just enough pressure on the topslide handle to cut. Then exert full pressure on the handle. Next, revert to normal pressure and, while feeding, lean on the tailstock. Then cut a further length with your hip pressing on the lathe standards, first at one end, then at the other. You will find that you have turned a series of steps in the work. This emphasises the importance (a) of using no more force on the sliderest handle than is necessary (b) *never* lean on any part of the machine while cutting and (c) develop a technique such that you always turn handles, put on cut, or manipulate the machine in exactly the same way every time. This consistency of technique is most important in all ornamental turning.

You must not assume that the machine will not need any more attention; it will, especially when undertaking any complex work. But at least it is now basically true, and any adjustments required will be detailed and minor, usually provided on the particular piece of apparatus being used.


### Driving the Machine

These lathes were all designed for treadle drive, and many practitioners prefer this to electric motors as they claim that they have both more control over speed and a better 'feel' during the cutting process; they can detect immediately any change in resistance and adjust accordingly. In addition, once accustomed to it, the treadle can bring the mandrel to a halt almost instantaneously. However, the majority of users now employ electric drive, one great advantage being consistency of cutting speed. A rear fitted countershaft is seen in Fig. 88, the motor being on the floor to the left of the standards. A drum type reversing switch is fitted to the left-hand upright. The countershaft pulley is machined up from mahogany, laminated from ⅜ inch thick ex-furniture wood, with a steel bush to take the setscrew.

The best drive is, in my view, round leather belt, although I have found long-spliced cotton rope equally good. Leather belt from ⅛ inch to ½ inch diameter is still available, but it may have to be ordered. I use both scarfed and glued joints (the glue coming from the local saddler) and wire hooks. Both are preferable to the hook-and-eye type of fastener, which are cruel to brass or wooden pulleys. For the higher speeds needed for cutting frames I use long-spliced cotton cord, 3 mm diameter, exclusively.

The mandrel pulleys on all O.T. lathes were grooved for gut bands, and the included angle is rather wide – 75 degrees is not uncommon. I cannot understand why this should be so; presumably the gut was crushed if a sharper vee was used. If an engineer's lathe of sufficient capacity is available it is well worthwhile reducing this angle to 50 or 55 degrees. On my Fenn lathe I machined the pulley *in situ*, rigging up a hand rest and driving the pulley from the treadle using one groove while machining the others. As to speeds, this is a matter for experiment, but my present machine, with a six-step pulley, offers 600, 500, 400, 350, 200 and 150 rpm, and can be run 40% faster if desired, as there is a two-step pulley on the motor. The higher speeds are needed for small work and for polishing, but I confess that I would have liked a lower speed than 150 rpm occasionally. The motor is ⅓ HP, and is more than adequate – ¼ HP will do. But I recommend that you obtain one with sleeve bearings rather than ball bearings, as the latter do make more noise. In which connection, you may find that an older motor is quieter than current ones which seem to be prone to very intrusive 'iron stamping' noise. However, the wise turner will retain his treadle and practise its use sufficiently often to make it a practical alternative. With it a speed range from about 20 up to 700 rpm is possible with the added advantage of being able to rotate the mandrel back and forth.

# 5 MANIPULATION OF THE EQUIPMENT

I do not intend to give a blow-by-blow explanation of the manipulation of even the most commonly used pieces of equipment. This would take far too long. More importantly, it would destroy all the interest and excitement of exploring the management of the machine and its accessories. I can assure you that you will spend many weeks or even months in fitting up the various chucks and cutting frames and finding out what they can do. However, any such exploration is the better for at least an outline map, and this short chapter will, I hope, help you a little on your way. We will start with the **headstock**.

### Dividing

The worst thing that can happen, and not uncommon at that, is to miscount holes on the dividing circles. First, check the index arm. The point should fit the holes well, and should exert a really firm pressure; you should be able to pull it out with one finger, and most can be adjusted by rotating the fixture at the bottom end. If yours is adjustable for height, set it at mid-travel. Now, Fig. 10, page 19 shows the index circles on my Fenn just after restoration. You will (or won't!) see that the numbering is almost invisible. Decades of Brasso have almost obliterated them. You can emphasise these quite easily. First, clean the face and then wipe it with methylated spirit, cleaning out the detritus in the engravings. Now spot each figure with black cellulose paint and *immediately* wipe off as much of the excess as you can. Let it set, and then re-polish. This will remove traces of paint on the surface without taking it out of the engraving. Despite this, the risk of miscounting remains, and I always mark the numbers I need for each operation with a felt pen – the type which can be wiped off. And, always make a list of the divisions you need, and check the marks as you use them!

### Segment Plate

This is sometimes referred to as the 'sector plate' (see Fig. 92). By setting pegs in two of the holes – there may be 60 or 72 of these – the mandrel may be rotated against these as stops, so that incisions

Fig. 92 The sector
plate on a Fenn lathe.

may be made as part of a circle on the surface or around the cylinder. Fine adjustment of the travel is made by moving the two screws in the stop pillar. It is vital that the pegs be a good fit in the holes, but unfortunately these often get lost. Even more unfortunately, the taper is not one of the modern standards. It *is* possible to make new pins fit, but my own solution is to recut the holes with a modern taper reamer and fit standard taper pins. These should be made with either a screwdriver slot or a cross-hole as an aid to release. The pins should be lightly lubricated when fitted. The usual method of rotation is by hand on the pulley, but the 'tangent screw' can be used as a slow motion drive with advantage.

### Tangent Screw

This is seen at A, B and C in Fig. 93. It can be used as a fine dividing engine, the wheel having 180 teeth and the index to the worm 24 divisions; as a stop, to lock the mandrel; or, as already noticed, as a slow motion drive. This is usually effected by fitting a winch handle to the worm-shaft, but it is not unknown for a pulley drive from the overhead to be used. Its use as a dividing engine is pretty rare, but it can come in handy when, for example, a second pattern on the work must be aligned exactly with a previous one. The tangent screw is used to bring the work into precise alignment, after which the vertical adjustment of the dividing index to the pulley is used to bring the point exactly to the zero of the dividing circle in use.

Fig. 93 (A) Tangent wheel; (B) tangent worm; (C) worm bracket locking screw; (D) collars for 'equal division of the ellipse' apparatus; (E) securing bolt for the 'spiral apparatus'.

### Thrust Collar

This replaces the guide bobbin seen in Fig. 93. On most machines this collar is keyed to the mandrel, and adjusted by means of the setscrew at the end. The adjustment should be such that there is free running, but zero endfloat – or as near zero as possible. Unfortunately over the years the adjusting screw wears, and will not stay put. LOCTITE 'Screw-clock' can be used, of course, but my own solution is to make a new collar in bronze such that (using shims under the head) the adjusting screw can be fully tightened at the desired running clearance.

In this connection a word about **lubrication** may be apposite. After many experiments with modern oils I have gone back to refined Neatsfoot oil. This is one of the 'oiliest' oils known and was, at one time, the basis for clock and watch oils. It does not go rancid like many organic oils. I am not sure that it would withstand heat, but loads and speeds on O.T. lathes are not such as to generate any high temperatures. You will find a note about this oil in Appendix II.

Fig. 94 Close-up of the screw bobbin and turret. The latter is on an eccentric bush.

### Screw-cutting Guide

This is shown assembled in Fig. 94. The guide or bobbin is attached to the tail of the mandrel in the same way as is the thrust collar, and the bobbin should be marked, so that it is always fitted in the same position. You will see that there is clearance behind it, so that the mandrel can traverse by about an inch; quite sufficient for most of the applications in ornamental turning, including the manufacture of chucks. The bobbin engages with a turret which has threads cut in six sectors or stations, each thread corresponding to one of the guides or bobbins. This is set on an eccentric bush carried on a bolt through the tail of the headstock. The turret can, therefore, be disengaged from the bobbin by turning the bush – you can see that this is fitted with tommy-bar holes for this purpose. The same feature is used to minimise backlash when the bobbin is engaged.

There are usually six bobbins in the set (some 'luxurious' outfits may have twelve) but all too often there is only one. My own had just that for the mandrel nose thread and no other. This is not a disaster (as long as the turret is there) as new bobbins are easily made, despite the very 'odd' threads used on these lathes. This is dealt with in Appendix I. However, both bobbin and turret must be handled with great care. The threads are a steep (50 degrees in most cases) vee form, with sharp root and crest, very vulnerable to burrs. On my own

I have rounded off the crests of both bobbin and turret threads. This has no effect whatever on their action, but does reduce the risk of damage.

The actual cutting of the thread is simple. With a suitable tool in the sliderest the mandrel is rocked back and forth sufficient to provide the length of screw desired. As mentioned elsewhere, this can be done by treadle, but I should fail in my duty if I did not warn you that this requires considerable skill; there is a risk of overtravel, bringing the bobbin hard up against the back of the headstock casting. This can be avoided by shortening the bobbins so that they leave contact with the turret before impacting the headstock, but I don't advise this, as there is then the risk of damage when re-engaging the threads on the return stroke. If you DO decide to try using the treadle then I recommend that you use a *hand chaser* (or 'comb', as it is sometimes called) on the handrest rather than a tool in the sliderest.

My own practice, where possible, is to use the universal cutting frame, inclined at the angle of lead of the thread, and to *mill* the thread, rotating the mandrel very slowly by hand. For fine threads – less than 16 tpi – there is no need to incline the cutting frame, and the vertical frame can be used instead of the universal. This method produces threads of very fine finish indeed and as you have absolute control of both depth of cut and rate of feed no problems arise.

There are few difficulties in using this device once you are accustomed to it. However, you may be puzzled over the numbering of the turret sectors and guide bobbins. These numbers correspond to Mr. Holtzapffel's 'standard' of around 1810, and are used throughout except for the feedscrews, which are all 10 tpi. Most other London makers used the same standard. (Many of them served their time with Holtzapffel.) Details are given in Appendix I.

### Sliderest

We have already covered the setting up of the rest in the previous chapter. Fig. 95 is repeated here to make things clearer. Notice first the operating handle, H. That usually found is a very nicely made steel one, but I found it too short to give the delicacy of control needed. I made the one illustrated from buffalo horn and filed down the stem of the original handle to fit a hole (about ¼ inch diameter) in the handle, which is fixed with Araldite. It makes a great difference, besides being rather more elegant! The two feed screws (L) and (M) are really depth stops – (M) usually has graduations on the knob or on the front collar which butts on the fixed stop-peg. Each division is 0.010 inch, and it is easy to interpolate to a fifth of this, if not to a thou (the engineer's name for 0.001 inch!). This screw is set to limit the depth of cut and

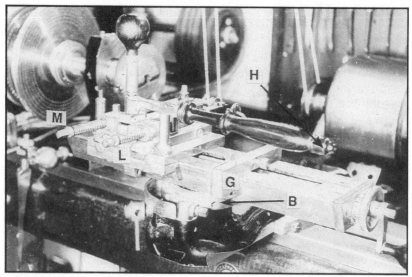

Fig. 95 Details of the sliderest.

locked. Cut is applied by applying pressure on the handle and with-drawing the right-hand screw (L) (some machines may have the two screws reversed.) This lever feed is a delight to use in every respect, and has the added advantage that you can whip off the cut instan-taneously should anything untoward occur!

However, many machines had an add-on accessory here, in the form of a hook which can be attached to the left-hand side of the slide. This hooks round the front collar of the screw (M) so that it can feed the slide both forwards or backwards, converting the sliderest to one with screw feed, like the topslide of an ordinary lathe.

Seen at (G) is one of the fluting stops, which limit the travel of the mainslide. Their use is obvious, but it is necessary to make sure that they are clamped up tightly. The winch handle can apply considerable force when magnified by the leadscrew, and it is all too easy to move the fluting stop a trifle each time the slide butts onto it.

One small detail well worth adding to the sliderest is not visible in any of my photographs – it is of the type with a registering cradle, referred to earlier. That is to drill and tap for a small setscrew, say 2BA, through the side of the cradle to lock the banjo in place. You can then slide the whole rest up and down the bed without losing the rest-to-lathe centres setting. A similar screw can, if it is not already there, be fitted to the height adjusting ring (B) (but with a copper plug at the end, as it abuts onto the threads) as without a lock here this ring has a nasty habit of moving as the rest is swung around, so altering the height of the tool.

### Curvelinear Attachment

Fig. 96 shows a very unsophisticated example of this device, fitted to the heavy metal-working sliderest from a Fenn lathe. You will see that an additional feedscrew is carried above the sliding member, with a follower (called a 'rubber' in the best circles!) which bears against a profiled master – actually, that used to make the horn handle in Fig. 95. Although very different from that usually found on O.T. lathes (see Fig. 96b) this arrangement will serve to illustrate the usage, as well as indicating possible arrangements for other machines. It may appear to be flimsy but it behaved very well in practice.

Fig. 96(a) A crude form of 'curvelinear' apparatus, which explains the principle.

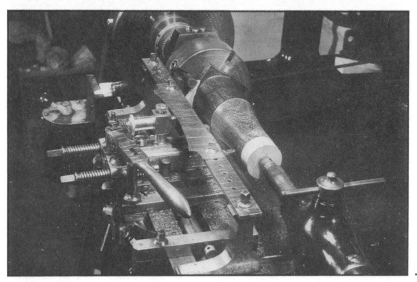

Fig. 96(b) Curvelinear in use forming the body of the peppermill seen in Fig. 121.

Before dealing with the actual manipulation I must say a word about the shape of the follower and tool. Fig. 97 makes the point. Unless the points of both are identical there will always be an error between the shape of the master and that of the workpiece. Fortunately, absolute accuracy is not necessary for ornamental work, but it is prudent to use a tool which approaches the shape of the nose of the follower. No. 20 of Fig. 63 page 64 is suitable (see also Appendix III). The second point to notice is that the tool may, at times, be cutting well down *either* flank, so that these flanks must be sharpened with as much care as the nose. Cutting is not, as a rule, taken from end to end of the template in one movement. Instead, cuts are taken from the largest diameters downwards towards the smaller sections on either side. Any attempt to 'climb' a steep section will almost certainly result in the follower jamming. In addition, it will be found that the tool cuts better when traversed from the larger diameter to the small. This is, of course, true for all freehand and most sliderest turning as well.

In use, neither of the two depthing screws is really necessary, as the depth of cut is set by adjusting the screw feed on the follower. However, I find it preferable to have both the follower and the right hand (depth of cut) screw in action on any but the simplest of profiles. It is also prudent – or at least, time saving – if the outline is rough formed by hand turning first.

After setting up, the screw on the follower is adjusted until the nose is almost fully forward – withdrawing the follower puts *on* cut – and brought into contact with the template. The tool is also adjusted to touch the work at its largest section. Both of these adjustments are, of course, co-ordinated so that the tool projection is reasonable. Then bring up the depth of cut screw (L) in Fig. 95, until it touches the stop. You can now carry on turning just as you would for any sliderest work. Withdraw screw (L) and traverse; the tool will cut until the follower meets the template, and automatically withdraw it to follow the curve. Work both ways laterally from the larger diameters, never 'uphill'. When finally the tool cuts along the full length of the workpiece you can withdraw the follower a trifle, resharpen the tool if necessary, and take a final finishing cut full length – though still working 'downhill'.

For profiles with very large differences in diameter I use the apparatus even when roughing. Setting up as above, but using a fairly narrow tool as No. 22, about one tenth of an inch wide. Move the follower *forwards* by about one tenth of an inch and then proceed to cut, but this time feed inwards only, without traversing, until follower touches template. Then withdraw and make another cut alongside, and so on along the full length. This effectively roughs out the piece, very quickly, and reduces the amount of work which has to be done by the profiling tool used to finish the shape.

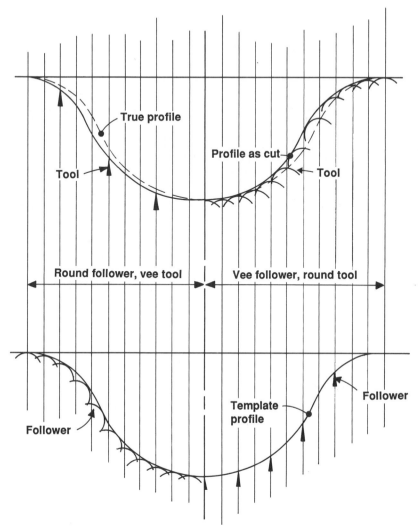

True profile

Profile as cut

Tool

Tool

Round follower, vee tool

Vee follower, round tool

Follower

Template profile

Follower

Fig. 97 Geometry of the copying template. Unless the tool and follower are identical shapes the cut profile will not be true.

The procedure mentioned above is used also when applying a cutting frame or drilling spindle to decorate the shape. However, I would advise you to practise on exercise pieces first. You will appreciate that if trying to set a basketwork pattern on, for example, a vase shape, both the depth of cut and the width of the incision must change as the diameter of the work changes. However, even exercise pieces are great fun – and often surprise you, in that it all comes out exactly right first time!

## The Tympan Chuck

You have not met this one so far! It is a device which holds a piece of paper on the mandrel nose so that you can check the setting of the machine to see whether the pattern you intend to cut looks right, by drawing it with pencil or pen first. Obviously a desirable procedure. The true tympan as supplied by Evans or Holtz is quite an affair, beautifully made of brass, and those who have them are very proud of them. However, this elaborate device is not necessary. Fig. 98 shows the alternative, which I have used for many years. A series of discs of paper – cartridge, or 80 gsm typing paper – is cut out roughly. The size is up to you, but four inch or five inch diameter is about right. Fix a piece of wood to a flanged backplate to fit the mandrel nose and face it flat, then turn the OD to the desired diameter. A second piece of wood – anything will do – of about the same size is also needed. Glue one piece of paper to the faced backplate, then clamp the other pieces to it with the second wooden disc, using fair pressure from the tailstock. Now turn the whole issue to a uniform diameter; you use a gouge or skew chisel (or both) for this operation, from the handrest, when the paper will cut quite cleanly. This done, coat the edges of the paper discs, still in the lathe, with gum or 'Gloy' paper adhesive or

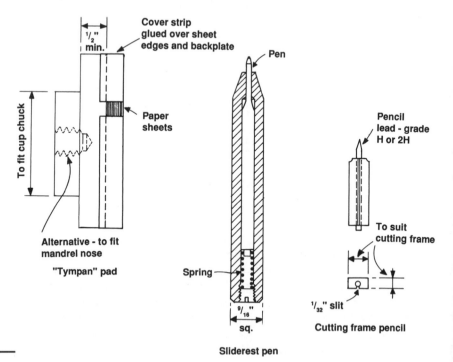

Fig. 98 A home-made tympan chuck with sketches of suitable pens.

similar, and stick a ribbon of paper round the circumference, but not right round; leave a gap between the ends of about ¼ inch or so. Once the glue has set the backing plate can be removed, and you have a pad of paper which you can fit to the mandrel anytime you need it. The gap in the cover slip allows you to use a penknife to peel off each sheet as it is used.

To write on this you need to make two tools, one to fit the eccentric cutting frames, the other to fit the sliderest for use with the eccentric or oval chucks. These are shown in Fig. 98 also. The small pen is drilled to fit grade H pencil lead; the larger carries the insides of a ballpoint pen. This latter must be dreamed up to suit the type of refill you have, and it is desirable that there be a spring somewhere, as shown, perhaps, to exert a slight pressure. The use of the device is self-evident, and I suggest that you set to and make one now, so that you can practise with the various cutting frames and chucks without using up a lot of wood! A tympan chuck by Holtzapffel is seen in Fig. 175.

### The Eccentric Chuck

We have already seen that ornamental turners base most of their decoration on patterns largely made up of circular incisions. The eccentric chuck will do just that, but can also be used to machine eccentric shapes, of which Fig. 99a is an example of some fairly fanciful ones. Fig. 99b is an example to show the procedure. There are six lobes separated by plain axles. After turning the piece to cylinder, the slide of the chuck is set over by the eccentricity 'e' and the nose index set to zero. The piece will now rotate eccentrically. The tailstock centre is brought forwards and very gently offered to the work until the point (which must be truly sharp) digs in enough to support the far end of the workpiece. Cutting starts at this end, making a lobe of width 'a'. The tailstock is then withdrawn, the tool retracted, and the chuck index rotated 60 degrees (for six lobes) after which the tailstock is again engaged in the new centre of rotation. The second lobe, also of width 'a' is then cut, and so on – working always from the tailstock end towards the chuck. Once all the lobes are cut, the eccentricity is reduced to zero and the tailstock engaged in its original (true) centre so that the little axles, width 'b', can be cut. Note that it is unwise to cut these axles as you go, as when working eccentrically there would be no line of thrust to take the tailstock pressure. In any case, it is more convenient, once the eccentricity has been set, to leave this alone, simply indexing the nose of the chuck for successive lobes.

You will appreciate that the thinner the lobes, and the smaller the diameter of the axles, the greater the skill required in execution! The variety is endless, as can be seen from Fig. 99a. That at the centre and

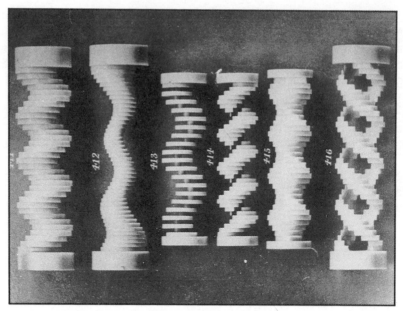

Fig. 99(a) Exercises in the use of the eccentric chuck. (*Holtz V*)

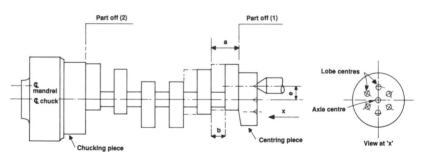

Fig. 99(b) Procedure when cutting an eccentric workpiece.

at the RH end have been bored through before eccentric turning, a well-fitting rod being glued (with weak water-glue) in the hole during the cutting. In the centre piece this has been replaced by a piece of blackwood after softening the glue and removing the original mandrel piece. (These specimens are all in ivory, about one inch diameter.) The RH example has been left hollow.

The execution of surface patterns is illustrated in Fig. 100. I have dealt with these in detail in Chapter 4 – this is just an illustration. But it is worth adding that **NO** drawing can present the full impression of the final appearance of these patterns. They are essentially three dimensional, and the reflection of light from the facets formed by the intersecting incisions is very difficult to photograph and impossible to draw. So, back to Fig. 100. A series of circular incisions eccentric to the main axis of the workpiece is required, as shown at (a) These are a mere repetition of Fig. 73 p. 87. The chuck dividing index is set at zero, and the slide adjusted to give the eccentricity, 'E'. The diameter of the incised circle is fixed by the radius, 'r', obtained by adjusting the position of the sliderest, which is, of course, set across the lathe bed. (The first operation will always be to face the workpiece.) A pointed tool, usually 90 degrees included angle, is used, and the first circle is cut; the depth stop is then adjusted and locked. The chuck dividing index is now turned – through 16 divisions to make 60 degrees in this case, assuming a 96 space dividing circle – and the cut repeated. It is then usually necessary to examine *both* cuts to see if they are deep enough, and to recut both if not. The process is then repeated until the pattern has gone full cycle.

ANY of the patterns described in Chapter 3 can be made in this way; it is only a question of deciding the relative values of 'e' and 'r'. A second row of circles could, for example, be cut within the first simply

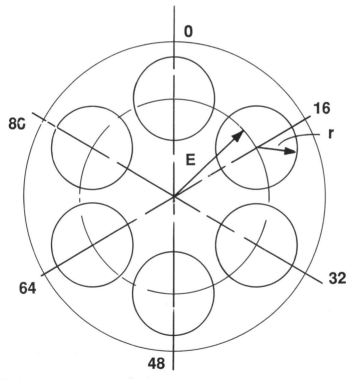

Fig. 100 A simple eccentric chuck pattern. Numbers are settings on the chuck nose dividing index; 'r' = sliderest offset – 'radius'; 'E' = chuck eccentricity.

by altering the eccentricity of the chuck. The vital precaution to take in executing this type of design is first to make a note of what settings you intend to use, and then to mark them off as they are completed (see Fig. 79).

You must remember that the workpiece is turning eccentrically to the lathe axis, and so is a considerable mass of the chuck itself. The out-of-balance forces can be very large, and vibration will result if the cutting speed is too high. The main reason for using an eccentric cutting frame instead of the eccentric chuck is that the cutting speed can be very much higher, resulting in a better finish in many materials. The second reason, of course, is that the whole drive chain – motor, countershaft, mandrel and chuck – must be brought to rest between each cut. Very time-consuming and tedious when a pattern may involve a hundred or more settings! Nevertheless the eccentric chuck is a very powerful tool, and has the great advantage that *very* deep incisions can be made, far deeper than is safe, or even possible, with the cutting frame.

### The Elliptical Turning Chuck

This has already been described, and you should refer back to Fig. 31 (page 38) to check details. The first point to note is that certain parts of this chuck merit exceptional care and attention. It is very important that the points of the two screws which attach the cam-ring to the headstock are preserved from damage. They are hardened, so that bending is unlikely, but they can easily be chipped. It is also important to ensure that the holes in which the points fit are clean, but take care not to 'ream' them in the cleaning. Take care of the threads on the screws, 'mm' in Fig. 31, too; these are deep vee form, with sharp crests, and any burr can cause trouble. It is worthwhile to stone off the very crest of the thread.

The cam-ring 'k' and sliders (or followers) 'jj' must be adjusted to run freely, but without slack. The cam-ring is of brass, and may well have collected burrs in the past. These must be stoned off carefully without forming any flats. The followers, being hardened, are unlikely to have suffered either damage or wear. However, you may be unfortunate and find that over the years the cam-ring has distorted – that on my 185-year-old No. 484 was slightly oval. This may mean no more than slight stiffness at two points in the revolution, and can be tolerated. However, No. 484 was quite serious. If you find this, unless you are adept at machinery restoration, I suggest that you seek help. The ovality must be stoned out, and this means painstaking work with marking blue, for the risk of overdoing things and forming a flat is to be avoided at all costs. The correction is not difficult, but it does need care and a lot of time, coupled with some experience.

The rest of the chuck is identical to the eccentric chuck in its arrangement and manipulation. To set it up the cam-ring is assembled to the headstock and the screws 'mm' adjusted until the line on the headstock matches that on the chuck. The cam-ring is now co-axial with the lathe mandrel – or should be. The forepart is then fitted, and it is advisable to do this by rotating the mandrel to enter the threaded nose into the chuck. We must now examine the geometry of the chuck, and this is where the tympan chuck comes into its own! Look at Fig. 101.

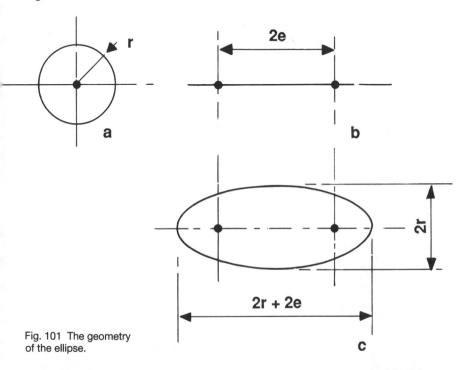

Fig. 101 The geometry of the ellipse.

If the cam ring is co-axial with the lathe mandrel, and the sliderest tool is set dead central, the tool (or pencil) will describe a central dot. Offsetting the mainslide will bring the tool over, and with the chuck at zero will describe a circle, radius 'r' as at (a). Return the tool to central and offset the cam-ring (the ovality or eccentricity) and rotate the mandrel again; the tool will describe a straight line of length equal to twice the cam-ring offset or eccentricity, 'e', as at 'b'. Now set over the tool to a radius 'r' and again rotate the mandrel. We shall see an ellipse. The minor diameter is equal to twice the radius 'r'. The major diameter (length) of the ellipse is equal to twice the eccentricity (offset of the cam-ring) plus twice the radius (offset of the mainslide). Try it and see.

Now look at Fig. 102. At 'a' a series of ellipses has been cut with a constant setting of the cam-ring, the eccentricity only having been altered by adjustment of the mainslide of the sliderest. At 'b', however, *both* cam-ring and mainslide have been adjusted for each cut, so that the lines are now parallel. To achieve this effect the ratio between the cam-ring offset (eccentricity) and mainslide setting (radius) must be kept constant. Thus, in making an elliptical box it is necessary to adjust the slide rest only if the thickness of the wall is to be uniform. Often this does not matter, but there are cases where it can be important.

Clearly we can superimpose elliptical patterns by using the index ring on the front of the chuck, as we did with the eccentric chuck. And, if the chuck slide is moved from the zero position when the index is so used, we shall cut a series of patterns round the face of the workpiece. An interesting effect can be obtained, too, if a series of ellipses (including the straight line) as in Fig. 102a is cut at one setting of the chuck nose index; and then an identical series repeated, but with the index turned through 90 degrees. Try that one, too! The possibilities of this chuck are considerable, and well worth a lot of experiment.

### Elliptical Solids

'Oval turning' involves rather more than the setting up of the chuck and presenting the tool to the workpiece. We must consider the

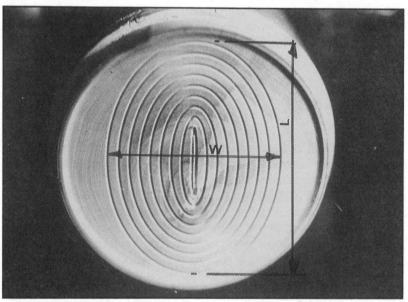

Fig. 102(a) Family of ellipses cut with constant setting of the chuck, varying the sliderest only.

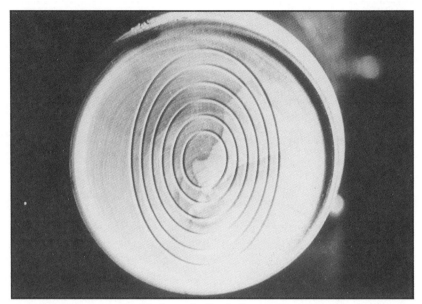

Fig. 102(b) Another family, this time adjusting both cam ring and rest; the incisions are parallel.

geometry of what production engineers would call the 'tool-workpiece interface' – jargon for 'how the tool cuts'. We start, of course, by turning a cylinder slightly larger in diameter than the longest axis of the ellipse and then machine the oval, and this involves an interrupted cut; no problem provided that you do not force matters with cuts that are too deep. But what about the situation when you have reached the oval form? Look at Fig. 103. This shows a tool with the normal 30 degrees clearance angle presented to an elliptical workpiece. At 'A' the cutting action is quite normal. At 'B', although the work at the point of contact is travelling vertically downwards, the surface is moving past the tool at an angle. The RAKE is negative, and the clearance angle has increased considerably. At 'C' we are back to normal conditions again, but at 'D' the rake angle has *increased* and the clearance diminished. This change in attack angle is continuous throughout the revolution. With some elliptical shapes the clearance CAN disappear altogether unless it is increased beyond the normal 30 degrees, and this fact must be kept in mind. My own tool outfit, which came with the machine, includes a few sliderest tools with clearance angles much larger than normal, obviously included for such work. Fig. 104 shows the effect when using an ornamental drill on the side of an ellipse. This has been exaggerated deliberately, but emphasises the point that careful thought must be given to the use of this instrument on elliptical workpieces.

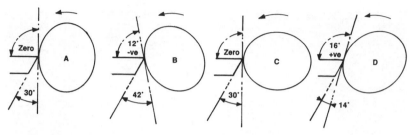

Fig. 103 Showing how the attack angles of the tool change when machining an ellipse.

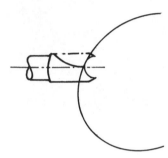

Fig. 104 The use of ornamental drills on an ellipse can be difficult.

Fig. 105 shows a parting tool set in front of a series of ellipses from which you will see that it would almost appear that parting off is impossible. This is not the case. Provided the clearance angle is of the order of 50 degrees there is no problem, although the appearance of the cut face is often interesting; highly polished, indicating the rubbing has occurred, but with curious patterning on the face. Machining a conical face on the end of an ellipse also produces an interesting effect – well worth trying out.

### Equal Division of the Ellipse
A little thought will show that if we wish to apply a series of decorative patterns on the face of the ellipse (or a basketwork on the cylinder) we cannot use the ordinary division ring if the individual patterns are to be an equal distance apart. The dividing circle will give an equal *angular* spacing, but as each cut pattern lies at a different distance from the centre of the lathe mandrel axis the spacing will change. This can be overcome by the use of a relatively rare accessory shown in Fig. 106. The two arms 'A' and 'B' are attached to loose collars on the lathe mandrel ('D' in Fig. 93) and 'A' is anchored at its outer end to the boss which normally carries the dividing index arm. It carries two gears

Fig. 105 A parting tool presented to an ellipse.

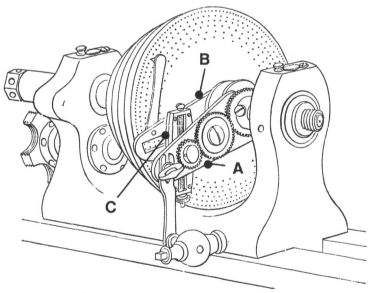

Fig. 106 The 'equal division of the ellipse' apparatus. (Fig. 93 shows the attachment rings and mandrel gear). (*Holtz V*)

meshing with one on the mandrel, in 2:1 ratio, such that the slide 'C' will rotate twice for each revolution of the mandrel. This slide has a leadscrew which adjusts a slider, to which is attached the second arm

'B'. If this slider is offset from the centre of the screw then arm 'B' will move up and down twice per revolution, thus moving the index at the far end. This engages with the normal division circles, so that as we index round in producing the series of cuts forming the pattern, the effect of the ellipse is automatically compensated.

In setting up, the two arms are first attached to the collars on the mandrel – small captive screws are provided for this purpose. It is then adjusted so that the slider arm 'C' lies *exactly* radial to the lathe mandrel when the chuck slide is either *exactly* horizontal *or* vertical. The two arms will then lie side by side. The slide must then be adjusted to take account of the proportions of the ellipse. With the chuck slide vertical the slider is moved, using the feedscrew, *towards* the mandrel in accord with the table below. The proportion is the ratio of the longer to the shorter diameter of the ellipse, and the movement is the distance of the pin of the slider on 'C' from its mid position. Note, however, that the ratio refers to that of the ellipse forming the centre of the line of decorations (where these are on the end face) and not the proportions of the body of the workpiece.

### Adjustment to effect an equal division of an ellipse

| Ratio | Movement Inches | Ratio | Movement Inches | Ratio | Movement Inches |
|---|---|---|---|---|---|
| 1.15 | 0.08 | 1.3 | 0.21 | 1.6 | 0.34 |
| 1.175 | 0.11 | 1.35 | 0.23 | 1.65 | 0.36 |
| 1.2 | 0.13(5) | 1.4 | 0.25 | 1.7 | 0.38(5) |
| 1.225 | 0.16 | 1.45 | 0.27(5) | 1.8 | 0.43 |
| 1.25 | 0.17(5) | 1.5 | 0.30 | 1.9 | 0.47(5) |
| 1.275 | 0.19 | 1.55 | 0.32 | 2.0 | 0.54 |

It is as well to check the division, using the tympan chuck, at the larger ratios. For ratios below 1.15 there will be little visible error if no correction at all is used – a ratio of 1.0 is, of course, a circle.

It must be realised that the apparatus is far less rigid than the normal dividing index, and that there may be some slack in the joints after many years of use. My own practice when indexing is to engage the tangent screw and to use this until the equal division index fully engages the desired hole. The tangent screw then takes all the cutting strain, which can be considerable when the ECF is used.

The alternative to this apparatus is to use the tangent screw. Fit the tympan chuck (or use the face of the workpiece) and then mark with pencil the positions of the centre of each item of the pattern, using the normal (circular) dividing index. Correct by sketching by eye-measurement the approximate positions which appear to give the desired equal division, and check these with calipers or dividers. Note the reading on both the tangent wheel and the worm index for each position, and use these in place of the dividing circles. This does take time – but ornamental turners are not paid on piecework!

### The Dome, Upright, or Spherical Chuck

To be accurate this is really a fixture which allows the workchuck proper to be rotated under the cutter, in the vertical plane through a full circle and in the horizontal plane through perhaps 300 degrees. It is NEVER used in rotation, as the out-of-balance forces would be too great, even at low speeds. The spherical shape, e.g. the domed end of an artefact, is first formed with the workchuck on the mandrel nose in the usual way. This chuck is then transferred to the dome chuck for decorating. Any movement needed about the mandrel axis is controlled by the tangent screw or the normal mandrel dividing circles, whichever is the more convenient.

Fig. 107 The dome chuck made by Mr. J.A. Batchelor in use (see also Fig. 162). (*Photo: Mr. J.A. Batchelor*)

Fig. 107 shows a home-made dome chuck constructed by Mr. J.A. Batchelor (shown in more detail in Fig. 167, Chapter 8) where an almost complete sphere is being decorated, using what appears to be a small clock-gear cutter carried in a Potts milling spindle. The sphere has also been decorated using the drills.

It will be appreciated that a *true* part sphere can be generated with this device, using the two rotations combined to turn the workpiece under a cutter in either the vertical or horizontal cutting frames – the approximate form having first been machined by normal turning methods. The eccentric cutting frame can also be used as if it is set at the correct attitude it will make a truly circular cut which passes both through the 'pole' and the 'equator' of a sphere. If the tangent screw is set to bring the chuck to 45 degrees from the vertical, and the work rotated using the tangent screw on the dome chuck, a true hemisphere will be produced. The chuck can also be applied to the decoration of flat panels on a flat-faced solid – square, hexagonal or octagonal columns, for example.

There are few problems in using it, the only important precaution being that you should assemble it to the mandrel nose by rotating the pulleys, not by screwing on the chuck itself. Clearance between bed and the chuck base is small, and this space must be kept clear. The body is quite rigid, and reasonably deep cuts can be taken without trouble.

### The Rectangular Chuck

As already mentioned in Chapter 2 this is, in effect, a vertical slide attached to the headstock mandrel, but compared with similar devices used on the saddle on engineers' lathes it is very much more versatile. Looking back at Fig. 34 you can see that the whole chuck can be indexed under the control either of the tangent screw or the mandrel indexing circles. The workchuck can thus be moved a total of four inches at *any* angle to the horizontal. In addition, the 120-tooth worm index on the nose allows the workpiece to be rotated relative to the chuck axis, this indexing facility being displaced from the mandrel axis by the amount of the slide movement. Finally, the mainslide of the sliderest can be moved horizontally across the face of the chuck. This gives 2 degrees of freedom in translation and two more in rotation, the latter being indexable over 360 degrees. To get a glimpse of how this may be used, Fig. 108 shows a rather crude test piece. After facing the blank flat, held on a woodblock chuck, the rectilinear is fitted up and the woodblock chuck and workpiece attached to the chuck nose. A profiled drill is set in the drilling spindle on the sliderest. The cut is started at (a) with the axis x–x horizontal and carried round to (b) by rotating the mandrel (centre at 'o') with the tangent screw. From (b) to (c) the cut is made by traversing the slide of the chuck, the axis of which is now vertical. The cut (c–d) is effected by traversing the mainslide of the sliderest; (d–e) using the chuck slide vertically again,

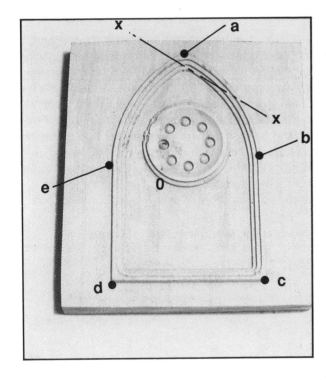

Fig. 108 An
exercise in the use
of the rectilinear
chuck.

and finally, from (e) back to (a) by rotating the mandrel. The whole process is then repeated using a flat ended drill, but with all the traverses increased by a like amount, to form the outside of the profile; after which the flat surfaces within and without the 'window' are recessed by simple rectilinear traverses of both slides. To achieve perfection the inside corners could then be attacked using a very small diameter drill (really an endmill) to give virtually sharp corners.

This is a simple example, and you will appreciate that preparatory work with drawings and a table of movements is essential if all is to come out as it should. The choice between effecting straight cuts with the chuck slide or sliderest can be important. You will also notice that we have not used the fourth degree of freedom at all. The possibilities are enormous, but it is *imperative* (if any complex work is to be done) to explore these on the drawing board (or your home computer screen if it has facilities for graphics!) first, then to embark on some practice pieces to refine the procedure before cutting in earnest. To encourage you I show on page 160 the famous 'Ivory Tower' made by John Jacob Holtzapffel specifically to demonstrate the powers of the rectilinear chuck. It stands 18 inches tall, and some idea of the accuracy of both craftsman and chuck is manifested by the fact that the ivory in the windows is so thin that light passes through!

### The 'Spiral' Apparatus

This varies in detail to such a degree that it is difficult to give much worthwhile information. And, after all, it uses exactly the same principle as the screw-cutting gear on an ordinary lathe. There are, however, two differences. First, the progression of the change wheels runs by factors of six rather than five (with a few extra wheels); and, second, it is normally used to provide pitches ('leads') greater than that of the feedscrew rather than the reverse. My own equipment has provision for two intermediate studs and has 16 wheels – 15, 16, 18, 20, 24, 2 × 30, 36, 48, 50, 53, 60, 72, 96, 120 and 144 teeth, and appear to be of cycloidal form, 20 DP. The main difficulty that can be met is that the wheels are rather large, so that interference can occur with some

## Table of leads using standard change wheels

| Lead, Inches | Ratio | Mandrel DriveN | Stud DriveR | Stud DriveN | Sliderest DriveR | Remarks |
|---|---|---|---|---|---|---|
| ½ | 5 | 144 | 72 | 50 | 20 | |
| | 5 | 120 | Idler | | 24 | Idler any number |
| ¾ | 7½ | 144 | 72 | 60 | 16 | |
| 1 | 10 | 144 | 36 | 60 | 16 | |
| 1½ | 15 | 144 | 72 | 120 | 16 | |
| 2 | 20 | 144 | 36 | 120 | 24 | |
| 2¼ | 22½ | 144 | 48 | 120 | 16 | |
| 2½ | 25 | 120 | 24 | 75** | 15 | ** May not be available |
| 2.566 | 25.66 | 144 | 30 | 96 | 18 | Approximate alternative |
| 3 | 30 | 144 | 36 | 120 | 16 | |
| 3.6 | 36 | 120 | 20 | 96 | 16 | |
| 4 | 40 | 144 | 18 | 120 | 24 | |
| 4½ | 45 | 144 | 24 | 120 | 16 | |
| 5.4 | 54 | 144 | 20 | 120 | 16 | |
| 5.766 | 57.66 | 144 | 20 | 120 | 15 | |
| 6 | 60 | 144 | 18 | 120 | 16 | |
| 6.4 | 64 | 144 | 18 | 120 | 15 | |
| 7.2 | 72 | 144 | 16 | 120 | 15 | Longest lead with one stud |
| 8 | 80 | 144 | 18 | 120 | 24 | + 60/30 or 30/15 on 2nd stud |
| 9 | 90 | 114 | 24 | 120 | 16 | + 60/30 or 30/15 on 2nd stud |

combinations, but this happens with ordinary screw-cutting chains sometimes, too! I give opposite a table which shows the leads which can (with one exception) be obtained using a simple train, i.e. with one intermediate stud. It is necessary to avoid using two studs in the basic train if 'crossed' helices are required, as one stud will be needed for an idler to reverse the movement.

The table opposite gives a fair range of leads, but it is quite easy (within the limits imposed by the gears in the set) to work out other leads. The 'Ratio' is the Lead multiplied by the pitch of the leadscrew; i.e. 10 × lead for most lathes, and with very little trouble suitable wheels can be ascertained by writing:

$$\text{Ratio} = \frac{\text{Mandrel } N}{\text{1st Stud } R} \times \frac{\text{1st Stud } N}{\text{2nd Stud } R} \times \frac{\text{2nd Stud } N}{\text{Feedscrew } R}$$

Where **N** indicates a Drive**N** wheel and **R** a Drive**R**, as in the table.

If an IDLER is interposed – i.e. a single, rather than a compound pair of wheels – then this will have no effect whatever on the ratio, but does reverse the direction of rotation. Direct gearing or a setup with *two* studs will produce *left* hand helix or twist; a setup with just *one* stud will cut a *right* hand twist. This applies whether the studs carry an idler or a compound pair. The determination of lead angle is dealt with on page 85.

We have already seen that the train must be driven *from* the sliderest, and that some resistance must be applied to the mandrel pulley to take up backlash. In addition, it is most important to check the running of the wheels for dirt and burrs on the teeth. In normal screwcutting, these, while undesirable, have little serious effect, but even the slightest roughness in the train will appear as a clear discontinuity in the flutes.

### Cutting Frames

The setting of these has been fully covered in Chapter 4. Some attention is necessary to ensure a positive drive when using the vertical and horizontal frames, as the tool suffers from 'interrupted cut'. I have tried several types of plastic belting and while these drive very well, their tendency to whip is a serious disadvantage. The braided nylon cord previously referred to is very effective, and is even better if treated with a friction compound. This used to be available commercially, but powdered resin rubbed into the braid does help. Some makes used rather wide vee grooves on their pulleys, and it is well worthwhile altering these to 45 or 50 degrees included angle.

The most important matter when using any of the cutting frames is the rate of application of cut. In most cases the use of these frames involves considerable repetition of movement and one quickly gets into a rhythm. However, it is most important that the withdrawal of the cutter should be accompanied by a simultaneous adjustment of the feedstop screw, so that the cutter cannot inadvertently be driven hard back into the next cut. I have got into the habit now of withdrawing the cutting frame by using this screw rather than the feed lever. This makes sure of the matter and at the same time ensures that the tool is withdrawn no further than need be.

Three final points. First, these cutters are almost invisible when working, and you *must* take care that they foul neither other parts of the equipment nor your own hands! Second, always delay starting on a complex pattern until you are sure that you can complete it – or at least a whole section – without interruption. Even if you mark off your worksheet very carefully there is always the chance of missing just one cut, and that can be disastrous. Third, both the drilling spindle and the ECF can get quite hot at the bearings during prolonged usage, and the spindle will expand relative to the body. Adequate lubrication is very important (but keep oil off the workpiece) and here again I have found Neatsfoot oil effective. But it is better to start work with the spindle very slightly tighter than you might like so that it runs without shake when hot, once work has been in progress for a while.

### Conclusion

Yes – I know that you will be disappointed, as it is almost certain that I have not covered the one point that has you completely foxed! However, the use of almost all this apparatus is reasonably straightforward and, provided that you take some time to experiment, you should have little difficulty with any of it.

# 6 A FEW EXAMPLES

I shall be showing a few more pieces in Chapter 7 but those which follow were all made on one or other of the ornamental machines I have owned – the Fenn, Holtzapffels 484 and 2456, and the Birch. None are outstanding technically or artistically (although I hope that they will bear inspection!) but I shall show a few pieces by others which may well astound you.

### Desk Pen and Paperweight

Fig. 109 shows the finished article, the base being of lignum vitae. The pen is a commercial article, of course. Fig. 110 shows the dimensions. This is one of the first pieces that I made, and carries a simple shell pattern of 16 rosettes, each of six cuts, using a 90 degrees included angle cutter. Although very simple the result is pleasing.

Fig. 109 A desk pen and paperweight in lignum vitae.

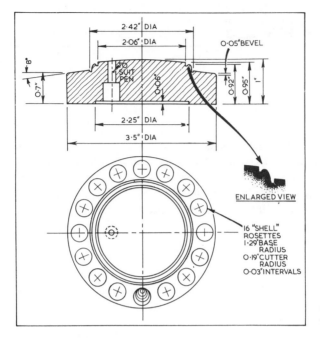

Fig. 110 Details of
the paperweight.

### Fluted Ebony Candlestick

This is a simple exercise in fluting. The base is plain turned from four pieces glued together to make a 'quartering' of the grain pattern – unfortunately this does not show in the photograph, Fig. 111. The fluting is done with the drilling spindle, using a half-round cutting edge, and there are 12 flutes on the stem, 24 on the socket, of the same width. Looking back it would have been better to cut say 16 larger flutes on the latter. Ivory rings are set between the steam and the other parts, these being screwed together using the traversing mandrel to cut the threads. The sconce was spun over a boxwood former, and has an extension which lines the socket.

### An Oval Box in Ivory

Fig. 112 shows a small box made from a piece of 'hollow' ivory on the ancient lathe shown in Fig. 7. The chuck is so true that the lid fits quite closely either way round. The ellipse is 1¾ins × 1⁷⁄₁₆ins on the body, which has relatively plain circumferential grooves at the top to match those on the lid. The hollow in the lid was turned to accept an elliptically turned piece of blackwood, but the bottom was filled with a plain cylindrical plug. There was very little waste on this piece, as the body is very close to the original shape of the tusk. Fig. 113 shows 'work in progress'.

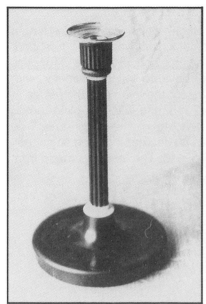

Fig. 111 A fluted candlestick in ebony.

Fig. 112 An elliptical box in ivory, turned on the ancient lathe in Fig. 7.

Fig. 113 Excavating the interior of the elliptical box.

### Ebony and Ivory Walking Stick

This, Fig. 114, was made on the Birch, which has greater length between centres than the Fenn. The stick itself was turned freehand, using damping steadies to reduce chatter and whip. It is 34 inches long, the diameter tapering from 1$\frac{5}{32}$ down to ¾ inch diameter, with ¾ and ⅝ inch diameter spigots to accept the knob and the ferrule at the bottom. The knob is seen in Fig. 115, and was first plain turned with hand tools, with decorative beading at the lower end. The barleycorn is deep cut, 3 × 16, with an 80 degrees included angle tool. This was done on the Holtzapffel, Fig. 116. The ferrule is made from stainless steel, quite plain.

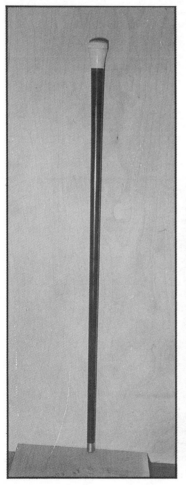

Fig. 114 A walking stick in ebony and ivory.

Fig. 115 The knob of the walking stick.

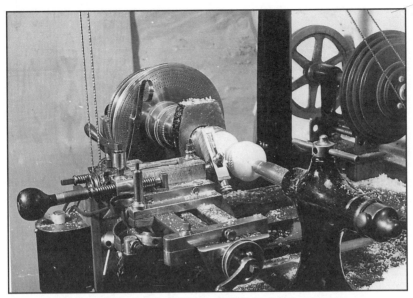

Fig. 116 Cutting the barleycorn on the knob. Note the tailstock support.

### Ebony and Ivory Pinbox

Fig. 117 shows the completed box, and Fig. 118 the drawing. You will see that the interior has a large radius at the bottom, to facilitate the extraction of the contents! The body is decorated with basketwork, but should have had 11 rows, not 10; I was still learning! A fine circumferential incision is made with a vee tool just below the basketwork, to match the joint with the lid above it. The ebony part of the lid carries a 4 × 24 barleycorn on the cone. The ivory is recessed into the ebony, and is decorated with a 6 × 12 barleycorn using the 144 circle. The knob initially carried a circumferential barleycorn, but this was not a success – it looked more like knurling – so it was machined away and a dodecagonal (12-sided!) outline generated with the ECF instead. Fig. 119 shows the plan view of the lid. Fig. 120 is the cutting of the basketwork, and you will notice that it is held onto a wood block in a brass cup chuck, using the tailstock for added support.

### A Pepper Mill in Partridge-wood

Fig. 121. The top and base are made from African blackwood, with an ivory knob. The sectional arrangement is shown in Fig. 122, but this, of course, must be adapted to the type of mechanism available. This drawing also shows the plain turned ornament, made with a pair of classical form-tools. The outline was turned using the curvelinear

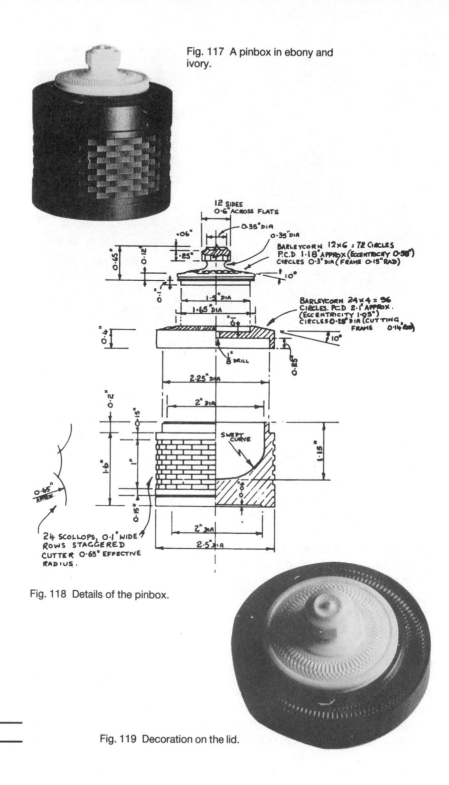

Fig. 117  A pinbox in ebony and ivory.

12 SIDES
0·6" ACROSS FLATS
0·35" DIA
0·35" DIA
BARLEYCORN 12×6 = 72 CIRCLES
P.C.D 1·18" APPROX (ECCENTRICITY 0·58")
CIRCLES 0·3" DIA (FRAME 0·15" RAD)
·06"
·25"
·65"
0·12
10°
1·5" DIA
1·65" DIA

BARLEYCORN 24×4 = 96
CIRCLES. P.C.D 2·1" APPROX.
(ECCENTRICITY 1·95")
CIRCLES 0·25" DIA (CUTTING
FRAME 0·14" RAD)
0·4"
1" 8 DRILL
0·25
10°
2·25" DIA

2" DIA
0·2"
0·15"
SWEPT CURVE
1·15"
1·6"
1"
0·65" APPROX.
0·15
2" DIA
2·5" DIA

24 SCOLLOPS, 0·1" WIDE
ROWS STAGGERED
CUTTER 0·65" EFFECTIVE
RADIUS.

Fig. 118  Details of the pinbox.

Fig. 119  Decoration on the lid.

Fig. 120 Cutting the basketwork, using the vertical cutting frame. The body is held to a wood block spigot by the tailstock centre.

Fig. 121 A peppermill in partridge wood and African blackwood.

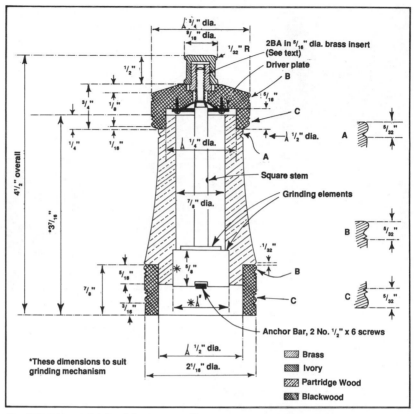

Fig. 122 Internal details of the peppermill.

apparatus. It could easily have been plain turned, but I wanted to get a bit of practice! (Fig. 96b shows this work in progress.) The only comment I need to make on this part of the work is that it was necessary to leave the body for several days after drilling out the interior before machining the diameters. I had to make two, as the first 'moved' so much due both to the heat that developed and to stress release on taking out the core that it could not be used.

The final turning on both body and base was done after gluing together, to ensure absolute conformity at the joint. The base has a 4 × 24 barleycorn on the 96 dividing circle, cut fairly deep. The cylindrical part of the cap carries a basketwork of 5 rows of 16, using a very narrow tool. The conical top has a ring of 8 shells each having 10 cuts. The chrome-plated brass knob supplied with the mechanism was totally inappropriate, so this was turned down to serve as a liner to the ivory knob. This has 16 flutes formed with the drill but unfortunately the pattern on the top of the knob does not show in the

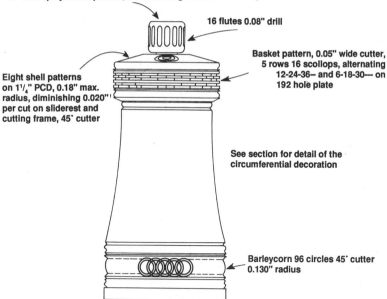

15 - lobe epicycloidal pattern, radius 8 flange set at 0.09" compensation zero

16 flutes 0.08" drill

Basket pattern, 0.05" wide cutter, 5 rows 16 scollops, alternating 12-24-36– and 6-18-30–– on 192 hole plate

Eight shell patterns on 1¼" PCD, 0.18" max. radius, diminishing 0.020" per cut on sliderest and cutting frame, 45° cutter

See section for detail of the circumferential decoration

Barleycorn 96 circles 45° cutter 0.130" radius

Fig. 123 External decoration. (See also Fig. 96b)

Fig. 124 The pattern on the knob, cut with the epicycloidal cutting frame, Fig. 47 (much enlarged).

photograph, so I have enlarged this in Fig. 133 – a single line forming a 15-lobe pattern. This took about half an hour to set up on the *cycloidal cutting frame*, and ten seconds to cut the pattern!

### Ebony Box with Ivory Fish

This box, which is 2⅛ inch diameter × 1½ inch tall, is quite plain except for a circumferential groove towards the bottom to match the height of the lid, but it is embellished with the fish pattern described in detail on page 101. The contrast is very effective indeed – a case where *lack* of ornament enhances the whole. (Fig. 125.)


### Three Ivory Boxes

Fig. 126 is the first major work in ivory which I undertook, and was rather extravagant in material. The body, 2½ inch diameter, was excavated by first drilling a centre hole part way through, then trepanning out at just under the inside diameter; and finally using an internal side-parting tool to bring out the core. This was used later for a smaller box, of course, but a lot of material was wasted by making the bottom solid with the body. The work was done on the Fenn, and at that time I had very few cutting tools. The body has a nine-row basketwork of 24 segments on the 144-hole circle, the tool being 0.1 inch wide. The lid is slightly conical with a flat centre. There is a ring of 24 shells on the cone, adjacent shells overlapping by four cuts, each having 11 rings. Within this, on the flat, is a 4 × 24 barleycorn of quite small radius – ECF set at 0.4 inch, with a 90 degree cutter. The centre is cut with a modified basket, No. 222 of Fig. 75 page 89.

 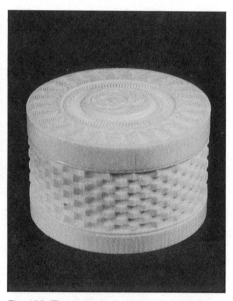

Fig. 125  A small ebony box with fish pattern in ivory.

Fig. 126  The author's first attempt at an ivory box. Basketwork and shell patterns.

Fig. 127 An ivory box showing the effectiveness of deep barleycorn on the body.

Fig. 127 is rather larger, almost three inch diameter. The body was made of a hollow offcut obtained at a sale, and the lid and base are from pieces of different tusks again, also obtained at a 'bits and pieces' sale. This led to slight difficulties with the fit of the lid, but over the years this has settled down. Ivory does move quite appreciably immediately after first machining and, to a much lesser extent, with weather and temperature.

The body has a deep-cut barleycorn of 3 × 32, the ECF set at radius 0.25 inches, and there is a circumferential 'architectural' ornamental bead on either side, which together fill the whole of the exterior. The ends of the hollow cylinder were, of course, formed with spigots to take base and lid. These are both slightly tapered on the cylinder to provide some balance to the slight barrel shape resulting from the deep-cut barleycorn. The lid, is, like the previous example, very slightly coned with a flat centre. The cone carries a ring of 20 shells so spaced that the outer rings of adjacent ones meet exactly – as in the basic ring of a barleycorn – and each shell has six cuts. Inside the shells is a shallow-cut barleycorn, 6 × 20, ECF set at 0.12 inch, and this surrounds a full and deep cut basket No. 222, Fig. 75.

Fig. 128 shows a presentation gift for a very special occasion, and was made from part of a large piece of tusk I had for many years but which I had not, so far, dared to show to a saw! It is, as seen in the drawing, Fig. 129, 3¾ inch diameter × 2⅝ inch tall, and was cut from the tusk as shown on page 81. Inevitably there was a large 'nerve' in the centre of the piece, so the centre of the lid was recessed to accept an ivory disc on the outside and one of blackwood internally.

Fig. 128 The 'rather special' box! It is 3¾ inches diameter.

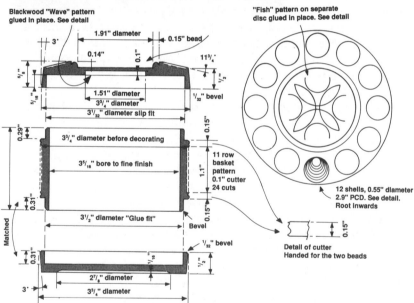

Blackwood "Wave" pattern glued in place. See detail

"Fish" pattern on separate disc glued in place. See detail

1.91" diameter

0.15" bead

3°

0.14"

0.1"

11¾°

0.15"

⁵/₈"

³/₁₆"

1.51" diameter

3³/₄" diameter

¹/₃₂" bevel

½"

3¹/₃₂" diameter slip fit

0.29"

3³/₄" diameter before decorating

3⁵/₁₆" bore to fine finish

0.15"

11 row basket pattern 0.1" cutter 24 cuts

1.1"

0.31"

0.15"

3¹/₂" diameter "Glue fit"

Bevel

Matched

0.31"

¹/₃₂" bevel

12 shells, 0.55" diameter 2.9" PCD. See detail. Root inwards

2⁷/₈" diameter

½"

¹/₁₆"

0.15"

3°

3³/₄" diameter

Detail of cutter Handed for the two beads

Fig. 129 Details of the parts of Fig. 128.

The body has an 11-row basketwork pattern of 24 segments and, as in most cases where I use this pattern, this is edged with a decorative beading from one of my form tools. (Actually, a pair, with left and right-hand profiles.) Both lid and base have a slightly tapered form which, although not shown on the drawing, is very slightly concave. The outer decoration on the lid is a ring of 12 fairly deep cut shells but machined with a half-angle 60 degree cutter – Fig. 130. This, with the complement of 10 rings, makes a very striking pattern. The recess in the centre was filled with the fish pattern, described in detail on page 101. The recess on the underside has a disc of blackwood cut with my personal design of 'Water Eddies', obtained by omitting two sections from the classic basket pattern based on the 96 hole circle – Figs. 131 and 132. The parts were assembled with 'Seccotine'. Fortunately the nerve in the base of the box was not unsightly, and this was left as it was.

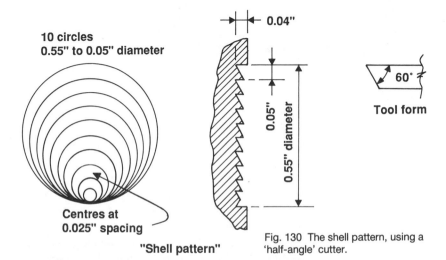

**10 circles**
**0.55" to 0.05" diameter**

← 0.04"

0.05"

0.55" diameter

**Centres at**
**0.025" spacing**

**"Shell pattern"**

60°

**Tool form**

Fig. 130 The shell pattern, using a 'half-angle' cutter.

Fig. 131 Top of the lid, showing the 'fish' and ring of shells.

Fig. 132 The pattern inside the lid, in blackwood.

### An Ivory Candlestick

The design of this piece, Fig. 133, arose from a mishap! After the socket had been formed and decorated the chucking-piece was then machined to form a further piece of ornament, when it was found that there was a large flaw in the ivory. This happens occasionally – I have a specimen with a musket-ball embedded so deeply inside that the animal must have lived for some tens of years afterwards – and the piece of ivory was well over 90 years old when I got it. However, the flaw meant that the original intention could not be pursued, yet the socket was so massive that any normal stem would have looked odd. As you see, the final solution was to use a combination of a single ivory pillar with a small colonnade of blackwood supports around it. In passing, I do *not* recommend the use of coloured candles, as they do stain the Ivory; nor that the candle be lighted unless kept under close supervision!

### A Ceremonial Gavel

Ornamental turners are always being asked to make gavels! I have turned them in almost every material, including just wood, but this one, Fig. 134, is rather special. The two heads each have a spigot fitted into the main body of the head, but with a 'washer' of blackwood intervening. The heads have a deep-cut barleycorn, but the handle is deliberately kept plain, to provide contrast. The block is of blackwood with a fairly thick ivory insert. This fits closely into the cavity to take up lateral stresses when struck, and so reduce the risk of cracking.

Fig. 135 shows the parts of another, plain turned this time, in ox and buffalo horn, before being buffed and assembled. The handle is a copy

Fig. 133 An ivory candlestick, the design of which emerged from a flaw in the ivory.

Fig. 134 A ceremonial gavel and block in ivory and blackwood.

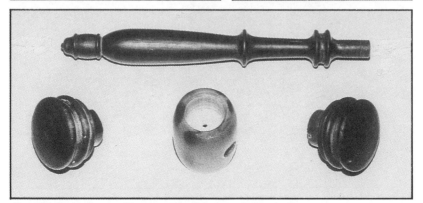

Fig. 135 Parts of a gavel in ox- and buffalo-horn, before buffing.

of the one I made for my Holtzapffel sliderest. Incidentally, most of the turning on this gavel was done on an old flat-bed Drummond lathe which I was overhauling at the time.

It would be wrong to illustrate a book like this with nothing but my own work, but unfortunately it is very difficult to obtain photographs of contemporary work, especially in ivory. To 'select' would be invidious, so I have included illustrations for which I have obtained photographs from the Society of Ornamental Turners. The **Condiment Set** by Mr. W.A. ('Bill') Jones is a very fine example of elliptical work, involving both the chuck and the equal division apparatus, Fig. 136. The strictly contemporary shape has been most effectively decorated with the drills. Fig. 137 is part of a **Chess Set** also by Mr. Jones. I suppose that every ornamental turner keeps a piece of ivory and blackwood by him (or her) so that 'sometime' they can make chessmen! The interesting thing about those illustrated is that almost the whole of the decoration is done with the drilling spindle.

Fig. 138 shows a **Golf Trophy** made by Mr. Fred Hayward of Bideford, a member of the Society of Ornamental Turners. The materials are kingwood for the eccentric twists and ivory for the base and top, although the golf ball is a real one. The machining of the columns is an example of 'eccentric turning' taken almost beyond the limit, as the centre of the 'twist' lies well beyond the diameter of the segments.

Fig. 136 A 'salt and pepper' set by Mr. W.A. Jones. A good example of elliptical work. (*Photo courtesy of the Society of Ornamental Turners*)

### Exotica

One day, perhaps, I shall find time to embark on a piece of work which will make use of all the facilities of the machine – a piece to 'Astonish Nations' as they say! However, it would be a pity not to show just a few examples of what *can* be done!

Fig. 137 An elaborate chess set, decorated mainly with the drills. (*Photo by Mr. Paul Bass*)

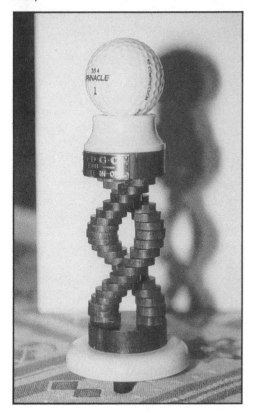

Fig. 138 A golf trophy in ivory and kingwood, though the ball is 'standard issue'. (*Mr. F. Hayward*)

Fig. 139 One of J.J. Holtzapffel's 'exercises'! (*Photo courtesy of the Science Museum*)

The **Pagoda** in Fig. 139 is remarkable for two features in particular. First, the extreme delicacy of the basketwork on the railings around the verandas. And second, perhaps even more remarkable, the extreme eccentric turning on the columns between the tiers. Close examination will show that each is a multi-turn helix of complete circular pads so eccentric that a rod can be passed down the centre.

The examples of **Slender Turning** in Fig. 140 represent a rather specialist aspect of the art. Some practitioners excel at it, but I should add that a rather special work steady is needed. However, if you examine each of these three pieces you will see that they include almost every possible technique, including the 'Chinese Ball', but in miniature. Note especially the four-thread spring on the centre ex-

Fig. 140 Examples of slender turning, part of Holtzapffel publicity material. (*Photo courtesy of the Science Museum*)

ample. To avoid misunderstanding I should explain that such artefacts are made in pieces screwed together, but even so they are something of a wonder.

The **Clock Tower**, Fig. 141, was made by John Jacob Holtzapffel II in order to illustrate the 'powers' of his newly introduced rectilinear chuck. Most of the work was done with this chuck in conjunction with the eccentric cutting frame, but both the upright (dome) and elliptical turning chucks were used for some of the work. The various windows, having been formed in profile on the outside were then thinned down

Fig. 141 The famous Ivory Clock Tower by J.J. Holtzapffel. (*Photo courtesy of the Science Museum*)

from within (on the rectilinear chuck) until the panes became so thin that they were translucent – see the close-up in Fig. 142. This amazing piece, 21 inches tall overall, can be seen at the Science Museum, South Kensington.

The piece shown in Fig. 143 is a set of **Interlocking Balls** made by Herr. Franz Kottek of Vienna for the 40th anniversary exhibition of the Society of Ornamental Turners in 1988. I assure you that these *are* made from one piece of wood, and that there are no hidden joints of

Fig. 142 Close up of the Tower, internally illuminated. (*Photo courtesy of the Science Museum*)

Fig. 143  A puzzle indeed! All in one piece, turned from a single piece of wood. (*Photo by Mr. Paul Bass*)

any sort! I can assure you also that the piece was made on a lathe – in fact, on the Holtzapffel presented to Prinz Otto von Hapsburg by Queen Victoria on the occasion of his wedding in 1886. But Herr Kottek *did* have to make some special cutting tools. How was it done? I don't know – see if you can work it out!

Fig. 144 shows a remarkable collection of 'Minarets' in ivory, also made for the Society's 40th anniversary (hence the 'XL' on the centre piece) which is the work of Mr. Paul Fletcher. These exhibits demon-strate the use of almost all the facilities normally available on an 'ornamental' lathe, but I have shown inset the detail of the base of one of the pieces. This shows very clearly the possibilities of the humble drill; in this case the judicious spacing of a profiled cutter had produced a very fine effect indeed. It is not surprising that these exhibits were awarded the Society's Haythorthwaite Cup.

Fig. 144 *Above*: a group of 'Minarets' made by Mr. Paul Fletcher of the Society of Ornamental Turners. *Below*: detail of the base of the centre Minaret. (*Photos courtesy of Studio Edmark, Oxford*)

# 7 ORNAMENTAL TURNING ON ENGINEERS' LATHES

Although true ornamental lathes are not as rare as many suppose, they seldom come on the market so much thought has been given to the use of the ordinary screw-cutting lathe as a substitute. In addition, suitable woods – and especially ivory – are obtainable only through specialist firms, so working in metal and plastic is gaining favour. The former does strain the classic O.T. lathe somewhat. They certainly can be used even on steel, but mandrel drives tend to slip, and the use of the ordinary cutting frames is possible only with the softer metals. With a little ingenuity almost any lathe can be used, although some of the facilities of an O.T. lathe will be lacking.

There is no commercial source of ornamental chucks, although a number of amateur-built eccentric and dome chucks have been made. They are, necessarily, smaller than those by Holtzapffel, Evans etc, but none the worse for that. The elliptical-turning chuck is, however, almost out of the question, although at least one has been made. However, as we have already seen, the greater part of current O.T. practice centres round the cutting frames, and the use of these presents no problem at all. The one major limitation of the usual model engineer's lathe is the centre height, at 3½ inches – seven inch swing – the size of work is rather limited; most O.T. machines are 10 inch swing, and quite a few 14 inches. More important, the chief essential for ornamental turning – means of dividing – is, nowadays, entirely absent from the screw-cutting lathe used by amateurs. It was not always thus, and those who are fortunate enough to own a Britannia or similar 3½ inch lathe of pre-war manufacture may well find that there is a set of dividing circles on the headstock pulley.

Let us look at this aspect first. There are two approaches. (1) to attach a dividing disc to the tail of the mandrel, and set a milling spindle on the cross-slide; or (2) to reverse the arrangement, and mount the dividing engine on the saddle and the cutter in the headstock mandrel. Either is effective, but I would recommend the second alternative, especially if working in metal. You then have the full power of the lathe available at the cutter – and can use the back-gear if necessary! However, I have used both methods on wood, ivory and metal, the choice usually depending on the type of cutter I wish to use.

There is a further requirement which, if not essential, is highly desirable – some form of travel stop both on the saddle and on the cross-slide. True, we have index dials on both the leadscrew and the cross-slide, and it might be thought that to be able to 'work to a thou' is good enough! But that is not the point. You may have scores of cuts to make to identical depth – on one of my pieces there were almost 500 such – and to have to *look* at the index every time would make it very slow work besides the serious risk of misreading the dial. Fortunately, this is an easy matter to arrange. Even a toolmaker's clamp will serve, but I show in Fig. 145 a cross-slide stop which I use normally for screw-cutting. One 'click' on the knob is 0.001 inch travel. Unfortunately there is no easy way to provide lever feed, but this does not matter a great deal. Let us look at some of these requirements in more detail.

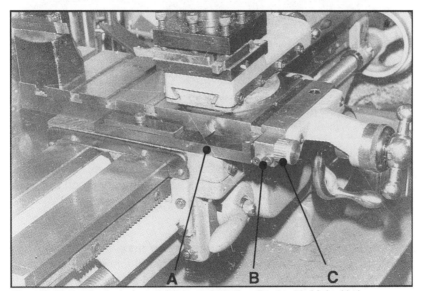

Fig. 145 The author's design of depth-of-cut limiter, fitted to his Myford lathe.
(A) Adjustable stop-bar.
(B) Threaded block attached to cross-slide.
(C) 40 tpi screw, head with 25 flutes; click spring below.

### Dividing

At first sight the ordinary dividing head seems to be the obvious choice, especially as they are available both commercially and in casting-set form – notably those designed by George Thomas and obtainable from Model Engineering Services Ltd. Obviously such a dividing engine can be used, but it is clumsy and very slow – and, again, there is risk of miscounting turns. On every count a *direct* dividing device is preferred. Again, there is available on the market a number of dividing discs which can be attached directly to the mandrel of a 3½ inch lathe, and others which rely on the 60-tooth bull-wheel, though this does rather limit the divisions. I have three direct dividing engines; one is a multi-row disc which I can fix to the mandrel of any Myford, similar to that available commercially from Messrs Chronos Ltd. One is a 60-division engine which is part of my Lorch equipment (Fig. 146) and the third relies on lathe change-wheels, built up from

Fig. 146 Dividing engine for fitting to the author's Lorch lathe. The plate has 60 divisions.

castings supplied by Model Engineering Supplies, see Fig. 147. (I have, of course, dividing circles on the pulley of the Lorch as well.) I prefer any of these to my 'proper' dividing head, being very much quicker.

### Cutting Devices

I use this term rather than 'frames' because none of mine would be recognised as such by the average O.T. practitioner! The first, used for surface decorations of the barleycorn, shell and similar patterns, is a normal boring head, Fig. 148. The small one is by Lushington, and the larger by the ABC company. Both are calibrated and I can work to 0.001 inch or 0.02 mm – the Lushington is metric. These carry cutters made up from round stock, some carbon steel and some in HSS. They are, if anything, easier to use than the normal eccentric cutting frame, and much more robust. Both have No. 2 morse taper shanks to fit the headstock, but these can be removed to fit other shanks, e.g. to match 10 mm collets.

The second is the well-known 'Potts' milling spindle, seen in Fig. 149. It can be fitted directly to the cross-slide, but I prefer to mount it

Fig. 147 'Model Engineering
Services' dividing engine, using
Myford change-wheels.

Fig. 148 Two boring heads, by 'ABC' above and by the Lushington Co. below.

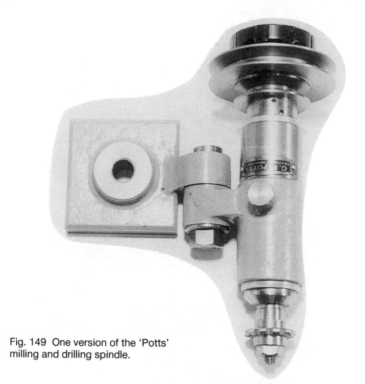

Fig. 149 One version of the 'Potts' milling and drilling spindle.

on the vertical slide. I use this spindle for drilling, either with twist drills in a chuck, or with a special collet to hold proper O.T. ornamental drills. And, of course, for profiled slot-drills. The Potts can, of course, be swivelled to act as either vertical or horizontal cutting frame, or set at an angle for helical flutes.

In Fig. 150 is the cutting frame designed by the late Mr. W.A. Bourne, former Secretary of the Society of Ornamental Turners. This very simple device is most effective, but I would prefer a slightly larger drive pulley. Many of these have been made by members of the Society. This, too, can be tilted at any angle and the spindle, 'A' can be made longer if desired, e.g. for decorating the inside of box lids.

I also have a more elaborate geared device, really a gear-cutter, which is part of the equipment of my Lorch lathe, and this may be seen in Fig. 151. I should add that Messrs Chronos Ltd market what is, in effect, a horizontal cutting frame, designed for clock gear cutting. It *can* be used in the vertical mode, but not as a drilling spindle. With care it can be applied to fluting work, but fly-cutting to cut basketwork patterns is just a bit too much for it.

### Cutter drives

In some cases the cutting spindle can be driven directly, from a motor

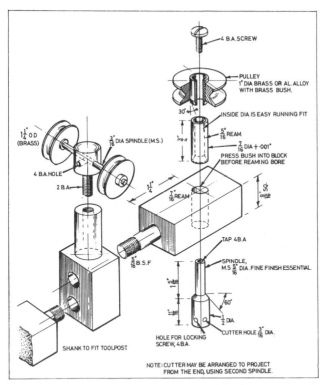

Fig. 150 Universal cutting frame designed by the late Mr. W.A. Bourne.

Fig. 151 A geared milling attachment on the author's Lorch lathe.

behind the lathe; it is, in fact, often convenient to mount the Potts on the back of the cross-slide rather than the front. Again, lathes like the old Britannia sometimes were fitted with overheads, as do many precision lathes. There is one on my Lorch. But it is very easy to rig up a drive; there is no need for anything elaborate. Fig. 152 shows one applied to my Myford. The pillar is a piece of one inch electric wiring conduit (gas pipe would do as well) which carries a peg at the lower end to fit the standard Myford hand-rest banjo. The cross-bar at the top is attached to a block bored to fit the upright, on which it can be locked in any position with a setscrew. The cross-bar carries a further block – which can also be slid into any position and locked – with a pair of ball-bearing jockey pulleys, source unknown; probably ex-aircraft surplus from years ago. As in the case of the Holtzapffel drive the motor is free-standing; at (a) it is sitting on the end of the lathe bed, and at (b) behind it. The motor is ¼ HP 1450 rpm and has a 5-cone pulley for speed variation. I use either 3 mm long-spliced cotton rope or ⅛ inch leather belt. This device has served me for years, and with the deep groove normal to the Potts spindle the saddle can be moved over a range of eight or nine inches without trouble. The column can be secured either to the saddle or the lathe bed.

Fig. 152 'Overhead' drive on the author's Myford. *Left* motor on the lathebed; *above* motor behind the machine.

Fig. 153 An ornamented brass box, 1½ inches diameter.

Fig. 154 Using the boring head and a dividing head to cut the barleycorn on Fig. 153.

### Some Examples of Work

Fig. 153 shows a 1½ inch diameter brass box, which has a fairly wide and deep cut barleycorn pattern on the lid, and a reverse helix basket pattern on the body, with a single row matching decoration on the lip of the lid. Fig. 154 shows the barleycorn being cut, using the Lushington boring head and a Myford dividing head on the vertical slide. The barleycorn comprises 8 × 8 circles (64 cuts) about 0.2 inch radius on a pitch circle of 0.95 inches, cut 0.055 inch deep. This left the pattern slightly below the top level of the lid. The body of the box was cut using a 1½ inch diameter slitting saw 0.08 inch thick, indexing 30 degrees to make 12 cuts to the circle, each cut 0.050 inch deep, which just went below the surface at the meeting points. Each row was indexed a further 6 degrees to give the desired helix. The slitting saw was run at about one tenth of the normal speed, to avoid any risk of chatter. A two inch saw would be preferable.

Fig. 155a

Fig. 155 (also overleaf)
Three brass candlesticks.

Fig. 155 shows three fluted candlesticks, (a) is a short one, the base having a single barleycorn pattern of 30 × 8, 0.4 inch diameter – the base is 5½inch OD; (b) has an overlapping pattern of 30 shells, each with 10 rings; while (c) has a barleycorn around the rim and 10 shells on an inner circle. In this case the barleycorn was cut deeper, and was 30 × 6, and the shells had double incisions, to make a bolder impression. A high-speed steel cutter was used, as the work would have been incredibly tedious at carbon steel cutting speeds. However,

Fig. 155b                    Fig. 155c

it was necessary to make a second cut – just a shave – after touching up the tool *in situ* to get the desired finish. Thus (a) involved 480 settings, (b) 600 and (c) 580! The Lushington boring head was used, with the base held in the four-jaw chuck on the Myford dividing head on the cross-slide.

The fluting was cut using a Clarkson FC3 ball-ended slotdrill held in the Potts milling spindle, the ⅛ inch diameter cutter running at just over 3000 rpm with a feedrate of about 1¼ inch/minute. Indexing was from the 60-tooth bull-wheel of the back gear with a rigged up detent made for the occasion. The fluted part of the socket was held on a stub mandrel in the chuck – the socket is made in parts – with plenty of space for the cutter to overrun the workpiece. Long chucking pieces were left on the columns, cut off later, so that here, too, there was sufficient overrun space. The only serious problem with these candle-sticks is the subsequent cleaning! Unfortunately the application of any form of lacquer spoils the inherent brilliance of the polished brass – and in any case, they still have to be dusted!

Fig. 156 is another pair of candlesticks, this time with helical fluting. The base is of Brazilian rosewood, the column of brass (they would have been even finer in German silver) and the socket of African blackwood with a brass insert and lip. There is an ivory ring at the

Fig. 156 Candlesticks with 'twist' fluting.

junction of the column to the base and the socket. The whole stands six inches tall. However, the main interest in the present context lies in the helical flutes, for no engineer's lathe, precision or not, is likely to be fitted with the indexing device found on the spiral apparatus of an ornamental lathe. We have to use an alternative method.

In this case the 'lead' of the helix was 60 mm (the Lorch is a metric machine) and the leadscrew is 3 mm pitch. The gear train used was 80 on the mandrel to a 20 × 90 wheel on the stud, meshing with 18 on the leadscrew; an overall ratio of $^{20}/_1$. There were ten flutes, and the indexing was effected by marking the wheels, as shown in Fig. 157. Two teeth are marked with a felt pen on the 20t intermediate pinion, and the 80-tooth mandrel wheel was marked at every 8th tooth. At the start, these two wheels meshed as shown in the sketch. After finishing the first flute the banjo was carefully eased out of mesh, and the mandrel turned to bring the next marked tooth on the 80 wheel between the two marked teeth on the 20. Care was needed to ensure proper (and, more important, uniform) meshing, but there were no problems. The machine was, of course, driven from a handwheel on

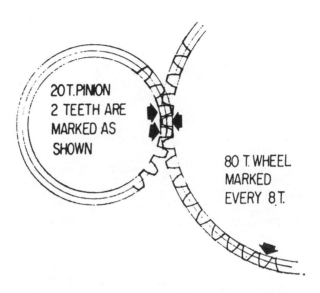

20 T. PINION
2 TEETH ARE
MARKED AS
SHOWN

80 T. WHEEL
MARKED
EVERY 8 T.

Fig. 157 Method of indexing a screw-cutting chain to form multi-start flutes.

the leadscrew. The one point which may need attention on lathes fitted with a leadscrew gearbox is the inevitable backlash in the box – that in a banjo train can easily be closed up. I get over this problem by hanging a leather strap over the chuck, or a round belt in one of the pulley grooves, and hanging a weight on the end. This holds the gearing in close contact all the time.

As explained earlier, if a rotary flycutter, or a wheel-type, is used this must be set over at an angle. The method of working this out has already been explained; in this case the inclination was 30 degrees, 12 minutes, near enough to 30 degrees as makes no odds! However, on later examples of similar work I used the FC3 ball-ended slotdrills instead of a wheel-type and there is then no need to incline the milling spindle.

My final example is not really ornamental turning at all, but is included to show how those without the curvelinear or copying attachment can achieve exactitude in profiling. The **Altar Cross**, seen in Fig. 158 was required as a memorial to one of the parishioners of a local church. It stands just under 14 inches tall, and is 7¾ inch wide, made of brass. The problem was to get the three shorter arms exactly alike in profile. Agreed, this could be done by free-hand turning by eye, but the slightest slip on one would be expensive both in time and

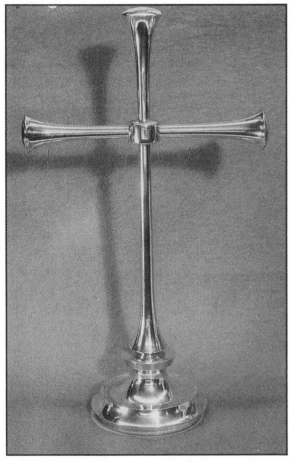

Fig. 158 A memorial altar cross, 14 inches tall.

material. The profile was, therefore, set out to co-ordinates. After much sketching to establish the design – although a wooden guide specimen had been supplied by the Vicar – the profile was drawn out very finely to a large scale and the diameters measured at intervals of ⅛ inch (the pitch of the Myford leadscrew) for about ⅜ inch of length near the large end, and thereafter at ¼ inch intervals. These ordinates would be accurate to a few thousandths of an inch, but to eliminate even such small errors the *difference* between the values of adjacent ordinates was tabulated, and these differences plotted against the longitudinal ordinates on squared paper. The points *should* lie on a smooth curve, and it was a simple matter to push any that did not back into line and then correct the ordinate itself. The figures that emerged were then used to determine the necessary infeed on the cross-slide to reach the required diameter – the largest diameter (1.3125 inch)

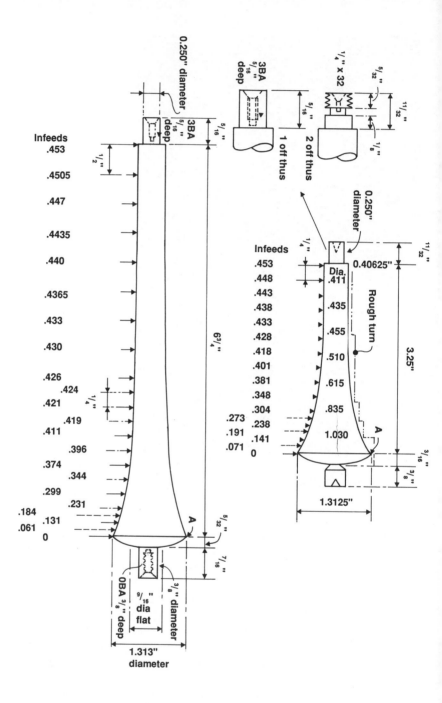

**Infeeds**

| | |
|---|---|
| .453 | |
| .4505 | |
| .447 | |
| .4435 | |
| .440 | |
| .4365 | |
| .433 | |
| .430 | |
| .426 | |
| | .424 |
| .421 | |
| | .419 |
| .411 | |
| | .396 |
| .374 | |
| | .344 |
| .299 | |
| | .231 |
| .184 | |
| | .131 |
| .061 | |
| 0 | |

0.250" diameter

3BA ⁵/₁₆ deep

⁵/₁₆

¹/₂"

6³/₄"

.273
.191
.071

⁵/₃₂

⁷/₁₆

A

OBA ³/₈" deep

⁹/₁₆" dia flat

³/₈" diameter

1.313" diameter

3BA ⁵/₁₆ deep

1 off thus

¹/₄" x 32

⁵/₃₂"

2 off thus

⁵/₁₆"

¹¹/₃₂"

¹/₈"

**Infeeds**

| | |
|---|---|
| .453 | |
| .448 | |
| .443 | |
| .438 | .435 |
| .433 | .455 |
| .428 | .510 |
| .418 | |
| .401 | .615 |
| .381 | |
| .348 | .835 |
| .304 | |
| .238 | 1.030 |
| .141 | |
| 0 | |

0.250" diameter

¹¹/₃₂

Dia. .411

0.40625"

Rough turn

3.25"

A

³/₁₆"

³/₈"

1.3125"

¹/₄"

Fig. 159 Use of co-ordinates instead of the 'curvelinear' for profiling. (The drawing should be read from the left side of the page.)

being the datum zero. These ordinates are shown in Fig. 159. This drawing also shows the chucking pieces left at the ends, leaving metal for the attachment to the centre boss – the arms were, in fact, turned between centres. The drawing also shows, chain dotted, the outline of the blanks after the initial roughing cut from bar-stock.

The blanks were then set in the lathe and steps cut to the exact diameter, each step terminating at the exact longitudinal ordinate. This could be accurate on both diameter and longitudinally to 0.001 inch, using both cross-slide and leadscrew indexes. After treating all the arms in this way they were coated with marking blue. They were then *hand turned*, using a large radius round-nose tool, with sweeping motions over the crests of the steps. This left bare witnesses of marking blue which became narrower and narrower as the final profile was approached, and it was easy to adjust the depth of cut to keep the witnesses uniform. When these witnesses had diminished almost to zero the tool was retouched and very light cuts made with a single sweep over the full length to eliminate all traces of blue. Fig. 160 shows the successive stages.

After screw-cutting the threaded ends, the chucking pieces at the large end were parted off, after reducing them to form the greater part of the curve. The final pip was about ⅛ inch diameter and smoothed off afterwards. The whole was then polished on a buffing wheel. I have

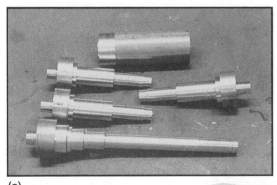

(a)

Fig. 160 Steps in machining the arms.
(a) The rough turned blanks.
(b) Co-ordinate steps marked with blue, one part-machined.
(c) Finished arms before buffing.

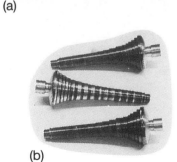

(b)

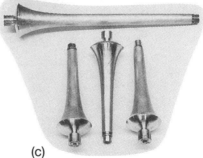

(c)

not dealt with the turning of the shape of the base which, apart from the initial work of metal shifting, was hand turned in the normal way; nor with the fixing of the arms to the centre boss (made detachable for ease of cleaning) as this is not a book about the manufacture of Church furniture! But the method of copying outlined above is very powerful and I have used it many times when identical profiles are needed, even though I have a curvelinear on the Holtzapffel. It is often much quicker to work out the co-ordinates than to draw out and make a template.

It will be seen that a great deal of work of a very satisfying nature can be executed on an ordinary engineer's lathe. The examples I have given are all in metal, but this is only because I use the ornamental machines on wood and ivory. But I have done work in both materials on my metal turning lathes, and even on a tiny Boley watchmaker's lathe; and, indeed, the ceremonial gavel in ox and buffalo horn (Fig. 135) was made on an old flat-bed Drummond lathe which I was restoring at the time. So, with a little contriving there is no reason at all why first class work cannot be done even if you have no 'proper' O.T. lathe. To encourage you, Figs. 161, 162 and 163 are photographs of an eccentric, a spherical and an oblique chuck made by Mr. J.A. Batchelor (a member of the Society of Ornamental Turners) to fit his Myford ML7.

Fig. 161 A home-made eccentric chuck, made by Mr. J.A. Batchelor for his Myford. (*Photo: Mr. Batchelor*)

Fig. 162 Dome chuck made by Mr. J.A. Batchelor for his Myford. Note the centring point on the backplate. (See also Fig. 107) (*Photo: Mr. Batchelor*)

Fig. 163 An 'oblique' chuck made by Mr. Batchelor. This is a rarity even in good OT lathe outfits. Note the depth stop (Fig. 145) at the left of the cross-slide. (*Photo: Mr. Batchelor*)

# 8 THE GEOMETRIC CHUCK

The geometric chuck is probably the most complicated and possibly the most interesting accessory ever devised for attachment to the lathe. However, I have no doubt that many readers will be asking 'What *is* a geometric chuck?' Put briefly, it is a device which, when attached to the lathe mandrel nose, allows a sliderest-held tool to cut extremely elaborate engravings on the surface of the workpiece. These can be and are developed to forms which it is difficult to believe have been made by any mechanical engine at all.

## Principles

Let us look at the principle first, and then go on to consider the mechanical arrangements necessary to follow them. We have already explored the capabilities of the eccentric cutting frame on page 89, and you will recall that it produces a pattern made up of circular incisions, and that there are three variables – the cutter radius (diameter of circle), the eccentricity (offset of cutter spindle from the mandrel centreline) and the number of divisions employed. Fig. 30 shows a fairly elaborate example with several different patterns arranged on a box lid. Now, suppose that instead of indexing the mandrel and making the incisions on the stationary workpiece we were to connect the mandrel to the ECF spindle through a train of gears. The pattern would then be cut on the rotating workpiece, and we should generate a continuous pattern in the form of a CYCLOID instead of a series of discrete circles. Fig. 164a shows the effect if the gear ratio were 12 to 1.

The shape will again depend on the cutter radius and the spindle eccentricity, but instead of the index we now have a gear ratio to control the third variable. Fig. 164b shows what happens if the ratio is 3½ cutter revs to one mandrel rev. The mandrel goes round *twice* before the line meets itself again, and we have seven lobes, of rather a different shape. Fig. 165 was drawn (using a pencil instead of a cutter) with the cutting frame geared to the mandrel with a *belt* drive, just to show the effect. At (a) the radius of the cutter (pencil) was altered leaving the eccentricity alone, (b) shows the effect of altering the eccentricity and leaving the radius fixed. The illustration, by the way, is a tracing of the original pencil line and considerable difficulty

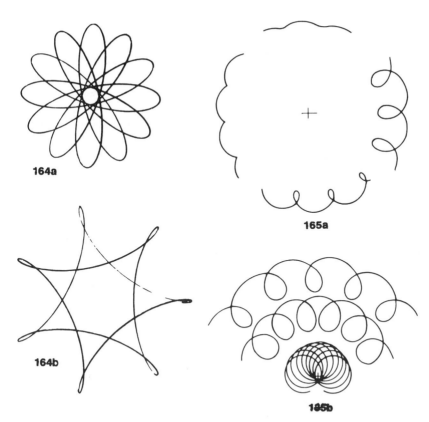

**164a**

**164b**

**165a**

**185b**

Fig. 164 (a) 12 lobed cycloidal pattern.
(b) 7-lobed pattern.

Fig. 165 Patterns formed by connecting an eccentric cutting frame to the headstock by belt.

was experienced with a belt-slip! Note that the centre pattern of (b) is almost a series of circles, but in fact all are a single continuous line.

What we have set up is a device which combines the motion of the mandrel and the eccentric cutting frame (two rotations) and the eccentricity and radius of the spindle and cutter (two dimensions). As each of these variables can have a number of values the overall number of combinations (and hence patterns) is considerable. However, the set-up is difficult to manage and the geometric chuck is a solution which puts all the variables except one (the final cutter position) within the confines of a single frame.

To take matters a stage further, it is evident that patterns in Figs. 164 and 165 could have been cut with a *fixed* tool if the work could have been rotated eccentrically to it using an eccentric chuck.

Now we are almost there for a simple geometric chuck. All we have to do it take off the dividing index of the chuck and substitute a gear meshing with one fixed to the headstock, when the work will revolve both eccentrically *and* coaxially with the lathe mandrel; this gives us the two rotations. One 'dimension' is given by the eccentric chuck, the other by setting the tool over on the cross-slide of the saddle. Naturally it isn't as simple as that – things never are – as we shall need a spindle going *through* the chuck so that the necessary gear-meshing can be on solid metal of the headstock. Further, and rather worse, we must have the gears so arranged that we can alter the slide on the chuck without putting them out of mesh.

This *is* a difficult one, but was solved a century or more ago by the use of the 'lazy-tongs' gear train. (There are other methods, but this one is the most common.) See Fig. 166. Here we have two gears, A and B, of which the centre of A is fixed but B must move sideways. Gears C and D are idlers. These gears are attached to spindles passing through the links E, F, G, so that the centre-distance between gears is kept constant. When gear B is to be moved, it is only necessary to slacken the spindle nuts slightly, traverse the slide, and retighten the nuts. The gears will have stayed in correct mesh throughout.

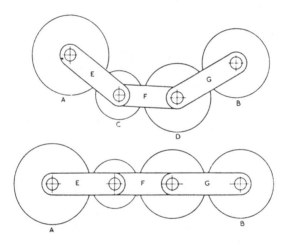

Fig. 166 Use of 'Jacknife Arms' to keep a moveable gear train in mesh.

So, by designing a simple eccentric chuck, with a gear drive to the nose-plate, a spindle passing through the body, and communicating to a train of gears on a lazy-tong, the last gear meshing with a fixed gear on the headstock, we have a simple 'chuck of one part'. (See Fig. 5, p. 13. It was done nearly 200 years ago!) We can elaborate a little, and provide a dividing ring on the chuck's nose, and also arrange for indexing to the fixed gear too, just to add a bit of variety.

So you want to go further? All you have to do is to make a second more or less identical chuck and fit it to the nose of this one, and you have a 'chuck of two parts'. Or three, if you like. Or four? Note, by the way, that a chuck of *one* part combines *two* eccentricities and rotations, a chuck of *two* parts combines three rotations and eccentricities, and one of *three* parts combines four, etc, etc. Those of you who have access to a computer may care to work out how many variations there may be assuming eccentricities variable in steps of 10 thou. up to 2 in., and with say 15 changewheels available in each part! I have no computer, but working it out in my head (it's much cheaper) my two-part chuck offers well over 20,000,000 variations!

### A Two-part Chuck

So, let us now look at an actual device. Figs. 167 to 170 show mine, which was made about 1910, probably to drawings published in *English Mechanics*, 21 October 1910. This was to the design of Mr. Plant, *c.* 1860, as modified from Mr. Hartley's design of 1850. It is unusual in being made of light alloy (most are of brass, and very heavy as a result) which has been identified as that used in the construction of airships by the Zeppelin company. It is a *two-part* chuck, with indexes provided both on the work-carrier nose and on the primary drive gear. There is a tumbler reverse, which reverses the relative direction of rotation of the base plate and the first part – this makes a drastic change in the pattern. In addition, a 'phasing gear' is fitted to correct for angular displacements which may result from variations in eccentricity. If you refer back to Fig. 166 you will see that when 'B' is moved laterally there is bound to be a slight rotation of 'B' relative to 'A'. This must be corrected if one pattern is to be superimposed on another. Superimposing 20-million on 20-million others makes the mind boggle!

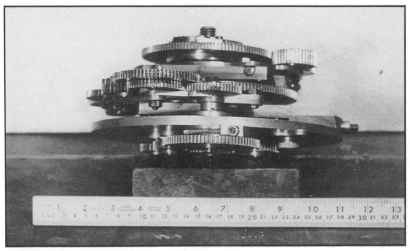

Fig. 167 Side view of the author's geometric chuck.

Fig. 168 Another view, with the two slides in line. The 'phasing wheel' can be seen bottom front.

Fig. 169 Underside view, showing the indexing circles and the tumbler reverse.

Fig. 170 Top view, showing the indexing wheel on the second part, and some of the change-wheels.

It will be easier to follow the construction from a drawing than from the photos, and Figs. 171, 172 and 173 are sketches I have made – more or less in proportion but not exactly to scale.

The main backplate, item (1), is 9½ in. dia. and is very securely fixed to the steel boss: this is threaded internally to suit the mandrel of the lathe for which the device was designed (see later) and these two carry the whole weight – about 15 lb. Forget the gears for the present. The first part slide (2) is carried in an aluminium vee-guide on the front of the plate (1) the slideways being seven inches long. The slide itself is aluminium, but the adjustable bearers are steel. The travel of this slide is 1½ in. and the feedscrew provides 0.1 in. per rev, with an index reading to 0.01 inch.

On the top of the first part slide (2) is attached a large diameter bearing, not visible in the drawings, which takes both journal and thrust loads. On this rotates the large 144-tooth gear marked 'M', which is retained by the bronze gear 'N' (36T) secured to the slide (2) by three screws (Fig. 172). The gear 'M' is thus the backplate of the second part of the chuck, and to it is secured the vee-guide (3). The construction is similar to the first slide – note the shape of the adjustable bearers in Fig. 172 – but has a travel of only 1.25 inch. The feedscrew also is similar, but as the head disappears under the slide in use the index is on the handle and not on the screw-head. I should have said that both slides have pegs fitting into reamed holes to

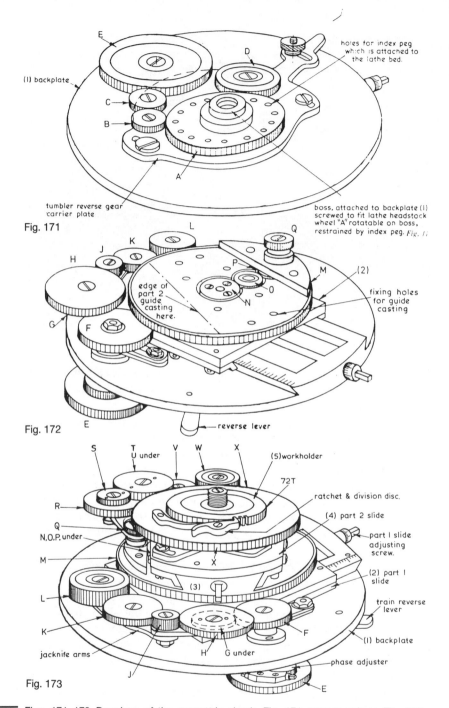

**Fig. 171**

holes for index peg which is attached to the lathe bed.

(I) backplate

E

D

C

B

A

tumbler reverse gear carrier plate

boss, attached to backplate (I) screwed to fit lathe headstock wheel "A" rotatable on boss, restrained by index peg. *Fig. 1*

**Fig. 172**

L

J K Q

H

P

(2)

edge of part 2 guide casting here.

M

O

fixing holes for guide casting

N

G

F

E

reverse lever

**Fig. 173**

S

T U under V W X

(5)workholder

72T

ratchet & division disc.

R

(4) part 2 slide

Q

part I slide adjusting screw.

N,O,P. under

M

X

(2) part I slide

(3)

train reverse lever

L

F

(I) backplate

K

H G under

jacknife arms

phase adjuster

J

E

Figs. 171–173 Drawings of the geometric chuck. Fig. 171 corresponds to Fig. 169; Fig. 172: view with top ('second') part removed; Fig. 173 corresponds to Fig. 168.

188

establish the true 'zero' eccentricity when setting up, and both slides have a scale of inches and tenths engraved on the adjacent frame.

The top of the part two slide (4) has another large diameter thrust and journal bearing, on which rotates a sector plate (only just visible in Fig. 173) carrying one end of the part two set of jacknife links and the large gear 'X' (120T) to which the workchuck holder (5) is fixed. This carries the 72-notch division plate and index, and a replica of the mandrel nose, to which the workchuck is attached.

### Wheel Train

Before dealing with the gear ratio aspect, let us follow the drive through using the three sketches. Fig. 171 shows the *back* of the mainplate (1) with its boss in the centre. The gear 'A' is free to rotate on the boss, and is held stationary *relative to the headstock* by engaging an index pin in one of the holes shown, (there are, in fact, two rows of holes available). Thus, when the lathe mandrel rotates the backplate (1) will go round with it, but 'A' stands still. As the idler gear 'B' or 'D' is attached to the plate it must go round 'A' and in doing so will itself rotate; it is an epicyclic drive.

The combination of gears 'B' to 'E' will be recognised as a normal tumbler reverse, and as 'A' and 'E' both have 80 teeth there is no gear ratio involved here. Behind gear 'E' is the 'phase adjuster', barely visible in Fig. 173. This is no more than a worm-and-wheel arrangement, enabling the rotational position of gear 'E' to be altered relative to its spindle. It is used to position a further pattern relative to a previously cut one and to correct for the effect of moving the jacknife arms.

The spindle of gear 'E' passes through the plate (1) and carries 'F' at the other end, and it will be seen in Fig. 172 that 'F' to 'L' are changewheels. (30 are available in all with a further 12 permanent gears.) Some, but not all, can be arranged as compounds, and a few are double-width. ('J' and 'L' are examples), 'H' to 'L' are arranged on a jacknife or lazy-tongs series of links, as previously explained. Incidentally, the links themselves are of aluminium, but also provided are some hard brass gauge-links which can be assembled with them to ensure accuracy of setting. These can be seen in one of the photos. The final change-wheel 'L' engages with the 144 tooth gear 'M' already referred to.

Fig. 172 shows the arrangement underneath the slide (3). The gear 'N' is firmly attached to the slide (2) and 'O' is in a bearing attached to the gear 'M', so that as the latter rotates 'N' and 'O' form an epicyclic pair and 'O' will rotate too. It acts as an idler, transmitting motion to 'P'. All these three gears are of bronze as they carry a considerable torque. The spindle carrying 'P' passes through a bearing to carry the wheel 'Q', thus making the drive available to the top of the second part of the chuck. It can be seen, just, in Fig. 173.

The drive from 'Q' to the final gear 'X' is again by change-wheels carried on a jacknife arm, and the arrangement is very similar to the first part. The main difference is that whereas the first part train is usually set up with, at most, one compound pair of wheels, the rest being idlers, there are usually several compounds in the second train.

### Movement Elements

We can now recognise the source of most of the relative movements of the tool and work. If both slides are set at zero eccentricity, and the tool is exactly on the mandrel centreline, *and* if both parts are locked rotationally, then the tool will cut a dot in the centre of the work. The whole mechanism rotates as one about the mandrel axis, and the work moves exactly as if it were attached to the lathe mandrel. (The same applies if the gear trains are brought into play, except that the work will rotate at a different speed from the mandrel.)

If the tool is now set eccentric – i.e. traversed by the lathe topslide – it will cut a circle concentric to the mandrel axis. Now let the first part slide (2) be given an eccentricity also. The tool still cuts a circle, but it will be offset from the mandrel axis by this eccentricity, and by using the dividing ring (5) we could cut a series of circles. The same applies if slide (4) is given eccentricity with slide (2) at zero; and if *both* slides are eccentric a circle will still result, but the position will depend on the combination of *both* eccentricities.

Now return all to zero, and then set a small eccentricity to slide (2) and a slightly larger one to the tool. Set the change gears of the first part ('F' to 'M') to give a ratio of 1 to 3½, but lock the second part (gear 'X') and set the second part slide to zero. The resulting pattern will be like Fig. 164b, although the exact shape will depend on the magnitude of the eccentricities chosen. (This alone gives a consider-able degree of variation.) The chuck is now behaving as a 'single part geometric chuck' and is, in this condition, quite a powerful instrument.

Leave the first part thus, and now set up a gear ratio in the *second* part (gears 'Q' to 'X') to, say, 1 to 21. 'X' now rotates 21 times for each revolution of 'M'. This is a simplification, as the 'epicyclic' first motion has an influence, but the effect is the same. Give the second part slide (4) a small eccentricity. The tool will now trace a pattern of one of the forms shown in Fig. 165 *superimposed* on that of Fig. 164b; and as one rev. of part 1 traces 3½ lobes, there will be 21/3½ = 6 small loops on each lobe of the base pattern. This type of pattern is the simplest combination available from a two-part chuck, and the art of designing patterns does require some knowledge of the principles behind such shapes, most of which are 'trochoids' of one degree or another. The results are often unpredictable even then – you must bear in mind that you are dealing with five interacting variables, and very small changes in eccentricities can have large effects.

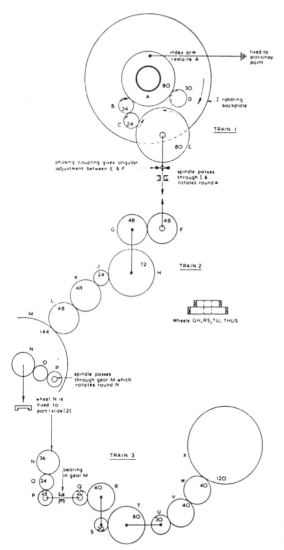

Fig. 174 The wheel-train through the whole chuck, opened out.

## Wheel Ratios

To give an example of how the change-wheels are set up, Fig. 174 shows the arrangement of the train as it was when I received the chuck. I have already mentioned that there are 30 wheels available – and some appear to be missing – so I have yet to investigate the full range of combinations! It will help if you keep Figs. 171 to 173 in mind when looking at this diagram, which shows the two trains 'stretched out' as it were, in a line.

As drawn, the tumbler reverse has 'B' and 'C' engaged, so that 'E' rotates in the *same* direction as the lathe mandrel, and this is regarded as 'forward gear'. In the first part the overall ratio is given by wheels 'H' to 'M' as, apart from the epicyclic effect, wheels 'A' to 'G' give a 1 to 1 ratio. The part 1 ratio is thus 144/72 or 2/1. In the second part of the chuck, labelled train 3, the ratio is 120/30 × 60/20 × 40/20 × 24/36, which works out at 16/1. Note that these are the 'tooth ratios' – usually recorded in the literature as the 'velocity ratios' though this is not strictly correct. The 'epicyclic effect' at the beginning of each train will add or subtract one from these ratios; i.e. train 1 and 2 together can be 1 to 1 or 3 to 1 depending on whether the tumbler is forward or reverse; and similarly train 3 may be 15 or 17 to 1, depending on whether 'X' rotates the same way as 'M' or the reverse. This depends on the disposition of the gears in the train.

It sounds very complicated, but provided one takes the same care in inserting compounds the right way round it isn't much more difficult than the setting up for odd threads in the lathe. The important thing is to keep a file of trial patterns drawn on a tympan chuck, so that time is not wasted in unnecessary repetition.

### Physical Details

The photos and sketches will give some idea of the layout of this particular chuck, and for the benefit of anyone who may wish to have a go at designing and making one the following details may be of help. (Reference can also be made to the *English Mechanics* article referred to earlier.) The gears are all of 20 degrees involute form, and are close to BSS 436. All are No. 24 DP (inch) pitch and ¼ in. face width, apart from the double width ones, which are really 1-1 compounds. The steel pivots are 0.343 in. dia., giving .0007 in. clearance in the ¹¹⁄₃₂ in. reamed holes in the gears. This is too much, and a closer running fit would be desirable. (Speeds are very low.) The spindle for gears 'E' and 'F' is ⅝ in. and that for 'P'-'Q' is ½ in. diameter.

The jacknife links are all ⁵⁄₃₂ in. thick × ¹¹⁄₁₆ in. wide, although some have cut-outs to clear parts of the mechanism. The link between 'F' and 'H' is not interchangeable, and therefore has to be slotted. All the gears except the three permanent ones 'N' to 'P' are aluminium alloy. This was a mistake, and making a new one I should use cast iron or a hard bronze. For reasons mentioned later the universal use of light alloy is not an essential, and I would make the slides of harder material, but it is worth having all parts above the slide (3)/(4) as light as possible; not because the speeds are high, but changes of direction can be abrupt with consequently large accelerations.

The backplate is 9½ in. dia., but in the fully extended position the slides need a swing of 13½ in. diameter. This means that the chuck cannot be used even on a 5 in. lathe and even if one were prepared to accept a 6 in. overhang from the mandrel nose. However, this is not a serious matter. The chuck, given a means of rotation, needs no other attributes of a lathe, and can be set up vertically as a machine in its own right. This is the way most chucks were set up from the late 19th century onwards. Fig. 175 shows an 'Ibbetson' two-part chuck made by Holtzapffel owned by Mr. K.J. Fowler, of the Society of Ornamental Turners, arranged in this way with crank-handle drive. The chuck is shown set up for drawing patterns with a pen.

Fig. 175 The late Mr. Fowler's 'Ibbetson' 2-part chuck arranged for manual drive. (Note that the 'tympan chuck' is in use.) (*Photo: Mr. J.K. Fowler*)

In my own case the chuck is used vertically, with a motor drive through worm reduction and gear drive to attain the desirable low mandrel speed (as low as 10 rpm.) The main problem is with the cutting point. Some of the more desirable patterns exhibit sharp points or 'cusps' and at these points the work turns instantaneously through almost 180 degrees. The shock on a normal vee-point fixed tool is considerable, and this not only leads to short tool life but may also cause a jerky appearance to the cut.

The last point of importance in the design and construction of such a mechanism is that of achieving and maintaining alignment. It is evident that even a small deflection at any point in the rotary or sliding bearings will lead to a variation in depth of cut. There is little problem in the slides and the bearings for gears 'M' and 'X', both of which are 3 in. or more in diameter, but the initial and terminal screw connections – designed on this one to match the mandrel nose of an O.T. lathe – are only $^{11}/_{16}$ in. Whit. and this is far too weak. These are being altered – at least so far as the work nose is concerned – to a screw-and-taper design which will ensure accurate alignment. The female drive socket is not so important, as after attaching to the drive this can be aligned and left alone once it is adjusted.

### Patterns

There is an acute difficulty in giving examples of the work done by the chuck, as the majority of the patterns – especially the complex ones – cannot be deeply cut and they are almost impossible to photograph without costly professional equipment. I can, therefore, only show some which have been drawn with a stylus or pen. Fig. 176 shows three made on my own apparatus. (a) is a simple circulating figure using the first part only – i.e. the second part of the chuck was set at zero effect. It bears a resemblance to a pattern of 32 overlapping circles, but is, in fact, a single line. (b) also resembles a pattern of circles but again is a single line. It is *not* two patterns superimposed! Both parts of the chuck are in operation, the first with a 'velocity ratio' of 2 and the second of 16. The eccentricity of the first part was 0.1 in., of the second 0.5 in. and the pen was 0.05 in. eccentric. (c) had the same eccentricities and first part ratio, the only change from (b) being that the second part ratio was 10/3.

Fig. 177 shows two exquisite patterns cut by Mr. Fowler on the two-part chuck shown in Fig. 175. (a) is formed by *superimposing* three identical patterns, each drawn at a slightly different setting of the dividing index on the nose of the chuck, (b) is a very skilful pattern indeed, being composed of eight superimposed lines, each differing from the next only by the adjustment of one of the eccentricities by

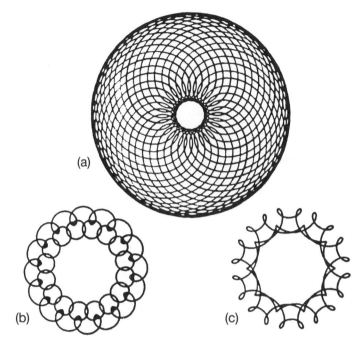

Fig. 176 Types of simpler pattern produced on the author's geometric chuck.
(a) With part one of the chuck only. This is a single line.
(b) A single-line 16-lobe pattern.
(c) 10 × 2 lobed pattern, two parts in operation, This is *not* a superimposed pair of patterns, but a single line.

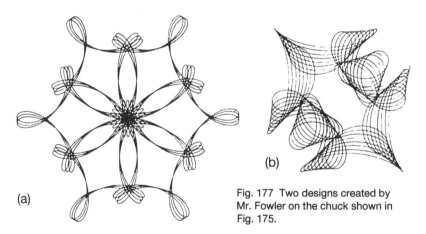

(a)

(b)

Fig. 177 Two designs created by Mr. Fowler on the chuck shown in Fig. 175.

about 40 thou. Cut on glass with a diamond (a not uncommon use of the chuck) these would be acclaimed in any company.

Fig. 178 is one drawn by the late Mr. Tweddle on a *three*-part chuck, and although it may seen unbelievable this is, in fact, a single line. In an

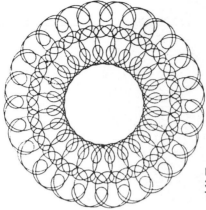

Fig. 178 An example of work done on a 3-part chuck by the late Mr. Norman Tweddle.

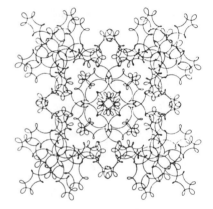

Fig. 179 Cut by Mr. Tweddle on a 4-part chuck, this pattern is formed of a single line.

example like this the excursions of the work-chuck seem to be quite random, and one goes cross-eyed watching it, but the final effect is remarkable.

The final pattern, Fig. 179, also by the late Mr. Tweddle (one of the finest exponents of the art in the Society of Ornamental Turners and the Society's first President), is made on a four-part chuck. It is difficult to believe that this is a single-line, drawn by a mechanical device, but that is, in fact, the case. As a line, of course, it lacks some of the artistic merit which would appear were it a faceted cut in the surface of a piece of ivory, but as a testimony to the skill both in setting up and manipulation of the device it must rank high.

### A Multi-part Chuck

Unfortunately I have been quite unable to find the photograph of the four-part chuck illustrated in *The Model Engineer* in 1950, and which was used for Fig. 179. But, thanks to Mr. Fowler, I am able to show Fig. 180, which appears to be a *seven*-part chuck, also built up by the late Mr. Tweddle. The centre section is a two-part Ibbetson chuck made by J.H. Evans; the top part is also an Ibbetson chuck, but made by Holtzapffel. Between them is a single-part chuck made by Fenn. These three make up a five-part chuck, the whole of which has been superimposed on what appears to be a further two-part chuck. The whole assembly is some 22 in. overall length; there are no less than 58 gears visible, and assuming normal construction there must be a further 36 or so not in sight. A formidable piece of apparatus indeed!

To conclude, I should, perhaps, say just a little about 'origins and availability'. My copy of Bergeron's *Manuel de Tourner* of 1796 illustrates a single-part chuck, and there is no reason to suppose that they were not available before that, even though some parts seem to be made of wood! The chuck designed by Mr. Ibbetson appeared about the 1830's and was manufactured first by Holtzapffel and later by others. There is some dispute as to whether the 'Plant' chuck was

Fig. 180 This remarkable assemblage is a *7-part* chuck assembled by Mr. Norman Tweddle. It is capable of at least $8 \times 10^{24}$ variations!

designed by Mr. Plant, or copied from that of Mr. Hartley, about 1870. The Plant chuck, in single- and double-part versions, was made quite extensively. Apart from these the majority of recent truly geometric chucks (as opposed to cycloidal cutting instruments) were homemade, possibly following the 1910 descriptive article. If they could be made by amateurs then, they can be now, and I hope that my descriptions may stimulate some readers to make the attempt!

# 9 CONCLUSION

During the time it has taken me to write this book, I have had quite a number of enquiries from people who have either seen some of my work, or read about ornamental turning somewhere, asking how they could make a start. Almost without exception they have commented that they could not possibly afford 'the prices which Holtzapffels fetch these days'. Let us deal with this matter straightaway. It is quite true that a fully equipped Holtzapffel outfit would cost quite a bit – but so will a fully equipped model engineer's lathe, and you have to pay VAT on that in addition! It is also true that some machines – a Goyen, for example – are so rare that they fetch 'collector's' rather than 'user's' prices. But, unless you are a collector, you do not *need* a fully equipped machine. If it has a dividing circle on the headstock and a sliderest you are in business; you can soon make, or have made, a cutting frame such as that in Fig. 150, or buy a Potts milling spindle, if you have no cutting frames with the machine. And a very simple sliderest will serve. That shown in Fig. 181 was all that I had on my Fenn to start with. Short travel, no refinements, and a leadscrew threaded 22.18 tpi at that! But it served me for some years and is still in use by a pretty experienced practitioner of the art. So, please do not be apprehensive about cost.

Fig. 181 The sliderest on the author's first OT lathe (Fig. 8). Though very simple, and rather short, much effective work was done with it. The drilling spindle is exchanged for the normal tool-slide when needed. See also Fig. 88, p. 108.

I have shown, in Chapter 8, how a normal engineer's lathe, as used for model engineering, can serve very well indeed. And, if you have such a lathe, there is no reason why you cannot make up your own 'apparatus' – see Figs. 161–163. Further, if you are then able to obtain an O.T. lathe quite without equipment – and perhaps needing considerable restoration – your engineer's lathe provides the means of both restoring the O.T. machine and filling in the deficiencies. In fact, I would go further. There are literally hundreds of five-inch plain wood-turning lathes lying unused all over the country. I have one, by the Britannia Co, which came from an Estate workshop. It is a very fine machine indeed, robust, with a good solid bed and a very rigid headstock. These are disdained by the present generation of woodturners because they cannot, as a rule, be run fast enough. But they can be the basis of a very good O.T. machine. Many have dividing circles on the pulley already but, it not, what of it? If you have a model-maker's lathe you can soon put this right; even a single 96-hole circle will suffice. Or you can ask a friend to do it – or, at a pinch, try the local College of Further Education. The opportunity of using their dividing heads for a job which is going to be of some use will be a welcome change for the endless exercises set before their students! So, try an advertisement for a 5-inch plain lathe in the local paper.

You do NOT need a Holtzapffel in order to practice the 'Art and Mysterie' – there are many other makers. Evans, Hines, Fenn, Buck, Munro, Britannia, Birch, to name but a few. But look again at Fig. 3. This machine is made of *wood*. So is the bed of my Holtzapffel No. 484 in Fig. 7. What is wrong with that? Many of the fittings for Waring & Gillow's furniture were made on lathes with wooden beds and, on one I have seen, the headstock itself was of beech apart from the mandrel and the brass bearings. The old practitioners of the 17th and 18th centuries had no other, and the work which they did is the equal of all but the best which has been done on modern machines since. So, if you keep an eye on the sales you may even find a headstock here and a sliderest there – and all you need is a couple of 'four by two's' in beech to make up a perfectly usable O.T. lathe! This is not as farfetched as it may seem for, even at Sotheby's or Christie's sales, such pieces of equipment do turn up at affordable prices – often together with a number of other odds and ends. As I have tried to show in previous chapters, the ornamental chucks are by no means essential. Most work today is done using the cutting frames, and these are easily contrived.

So, my message is – 'If you are interested, just get started with what you have'. If you have nothing, then aim at the minimum of necessities. I have seen quite presentable work done on a modified ADEPT lathe – and you cannot find much simpler than that!

# APPENDIX I   HOLTZAPFFEL SCREW THREADS

The threads were originated by Holtzapffel in 1794–5, and standardised in the years 1796–1804. From 1820 most lead and guide-screws were changed to 10tpi, and after about 1850 all screws and nuts above ½ in. dia. (except the mandrel nose thread) were changed to aliquot threads.

When making replacement screws, the original must be examined to see whether it is of the 'deep' 50 degrees angle or 'shallow' 60 degrees angle thread form. The pitches below ½ in. and the 9.45 nose thread were used until 1924.

The 'screw hob' mentioned in the table is the guide bobbin on traversing mandrel screw-cutting lathes, page 23. The 'tap mark' was used on taps and dies.

| Tap Mark Letter | Dia. in | Thread No. | TPI | Hob No. | Tap Mark Letter | Dia in | Thread No. | TPI | Hob No. |
|---|---|---|---|---|---|---|---|---|---|
| A | 1.00 | 1 | 6.58 | | K | ¼ | 8 | 25.71 | 5 |
| B | 0.875 | 2 | 8.25 | | L | 0.24 | 10 | 36.10 | 6 |
| C | ¾ | 3 | 9.45 | 1 | M | 0.21 | 9 | 28.88 | |
| D₁ | ⅝ | 4 | 13.09 | 2 | N | 0.20 | 10 | 36.10 | |
| D₂ | ⁹⁄₁₆ | 4 | 13.09 | 2 | O | 0.18½ | 11 | 39.83 | |
| E | ½ | 4 | 13.09 | 2 | P | 0.18 | 10 | 36.10 | |
| F | 0.45 | 5 | 16.5 | 3 | Q | 0.16¼ | 11 | 39.83 | |
| G | 0.41 | 6 | 19.89 | 4 | R | 0.15 | 12 | 55.11 | |
| H | 0.36 | 6 | 19.89 | 4 | S | 0.13½ | 12 | 55.11 | |
| – | – | 7 | 22.12 | | T | 0.12 | 12 | 55.11 | |
| I | 0.33 | 8 | 25.71 | 5 | U | 0.10 | 12 | 55.11 | |
| J | 0.29 | 8 | 25.71 | 5 | | | | | |

Thread heights. 'Deep' = 1.072P. 'Shallow' = 0.866P. Crest and root is a sharp point.

## Screwcutting Holtzapffel Threads

The following are for a MYFORD lathe *with gearbox*, and 8 tpi lead-

| Holtz tpi | Gearbox set tpi | Mandrel wheel | First stud Drive R | First stud Drive N | Second Drive R | Second Drive N | Leadscrew wheel | Actual pitch | Error |
|---|---|---|---|---|---|---|---|---|---|
| 6.58 | 14 | 50 | 47 | 60 | IDLER(55) | | 30 | 6.580 | none |
| 8.25 | 11 | 60 | ——— ANY IDLERS ——— | | | | 45 | 8.250 | none |
| 9.45 | 8 | 40 | IDLER(50) | | 45 | 40 | 42 | 9.450 | none |
| | | or 60 | IDLER(50) | | 45 | 40 | 63 | 9.450 | none |
| 13.09 | 11 | 30 | 51 | 60 | IDLER(50) | | 42 | 13.090 | none |
| 16.5 | 11 | 40 | ——— IDLERS ——— | | | | 60 | 16.500 | none |
| 19.89 | 9 | 50 | 65 | 30 | IDLER(60) | | 51 | 19.890 | none |
| 22.12 | 16 | 50 | IDLER(55) | | 35 | 38 | 75 | 22.105 | 0.000031"/in. |
| 25.71 | 20 | 27 | ——— IDLERS ——— | | | | 21 | 25.714 | 0.000006"/in. |
| 28.88 | 16 | 50 | 38 | 40 | 38 | 30 | 75 | 28.880 | none |
| 36.1 | 19 | 30 | ——— IDLERS ——— | | | | 57 | 36.100 | none |
| 39.83 | 14 | 37 | IDLER(65) | | 25 | 75 | 39 | 39.8461 | 0.0004"/in. |
| 55.11 | 26 | 53 | ——— IDLERS ——— | | | | 25 | 55.12 | 0.0002"/in. |

screw, but can be used with change-wheels as follows; where 8 tpi is called for in column 2, set up as shown; for 16 tpi use 25T on the mandrel; for others, set up additional wheels to cut the Col. 3 thread in place of idlers in the chain. The half-nuts MUST remain engaged throughout for all threads.

There has been much debate in the past on the possible origins of these unusual pitches, the general opinion then being that they were related to one of the many 'continental' inches used in Europe up until the mid-19th century. A little examination shows, however, that there is no rational connection between the pitches and any of these inches. However, it should be remembered that these threads were originated around 1795, and the methods used to generate them in the first place, and the subsequent correction of both incremental error and thread 'drunkenness', would lead inevitably to some deviation from the design pitch. Looking at the figures it will be seen that most are within the odd per cent of a perfectly rational figure – bearing in mind that threads were not, in those days, related to decimals of the inch (in those days the inch was normally divided into 12ths and 144ths!). Taking all things into account it seems likely that the original design threads were intended to be 6½, 8, 9½, 13, 16, 20, 22, 25, 30, 36, 40 and 55 tpi. The final figures are all within 4% of this, most of them are much closer. Similar arguments apply to some of the unusual screw diameters. Tap 'G' for example, approximates to $5/12$ inch dia. 'I' is $4/12$ and 'M' is $2½/12$. The table on p. 201 is a copy of an original manuscript headed *Dimensions of H & Co's screw threads*, found in a box of fittings. The 'fractional decimals' suggest that H & Co's micrometer or vernier read only to hundredths of an inch.

# APPENDIX II  NEATSFOOT OIL

Some difficulty may be experienced in obtaining **refined** neatsfoot oil in this country, as there is not a great deal of use for it, but raw neatsfoot *is* sold by saddlers and some veterinary chemists. A long account of its purification – down to watch and clock oil – is given in Volume I of Holtzapffel's *Turning and Mechanical Manipulation* and I have adapted this method to provide my own supplies.

The raw oil should be taken, if possible, from a new drum, without stirring up the contents too much, as a fatty deposit is precipitated in storage. If any is present when you get it home this can be strained out through a muslin cloth. Don't throw it away – it is very useful for coating seldom-used tools. Set the oil in clear glass bottles, and expose them to sunlight for a whole summer if possible. Note that it is the ultra-violet light and cosmic rays which 'do the business' not the heat. Though my own bottles live in the greenhouse, they would be better out of doors, as this avoids two thicknesses of glass. When the cold weather arrives a thick deposit of fat will form in the bottom of the bottle. Decant off the clear liquid into further clear glass bottles. (The fat will melt when it gets warm, so decant while still cold.)

The clear oil is quite usable, and I always keep a bottle of this 'first brew'. However, a further summer exposed to sunlight followed by decanting when cold will produce a better quality still, and this second brew I use on the lathe. As a rule a third exposure produces very little deposit, and I have never gone any further.

Neatsfoot makes quite a good cutting oil – for which purpose the unrefined material can be used – and I have found that it can help a little when cutting the occasional sample of ivory which is heavily patterned in the tusk, this usually means that it is a bit 'grainy'. Overall it is a very good lubricant in cases where a very 'slippery' oil is needed and as it does not go rancid it has many other applications.

# APPENDIX III  THE CONSTRUCTION OF TEMPLATES FOR THE 'CURVELINEAR' APPARATUS

As mentioned on p. 123, slight inaccuracies caused by the difference between the profiles of the tool and the follower are seldom important. However, there are occasions when an exact shape is needed. This can be obtained by a simple construction, as shown in the sketch, Fig. 182. The procedure is as follows.

(1) Draw out the exact shape required, full size or larger.
(2) Draw a series of ordinates at right angles to the axis of the workpiece. A spacing of about ¼ inch is suitable, but should be closer in places where there may be sudden changes of shape.
(3) With centres on these ordinates draw radii which just touch the desired outline, the radius being that of the planform of the tool.

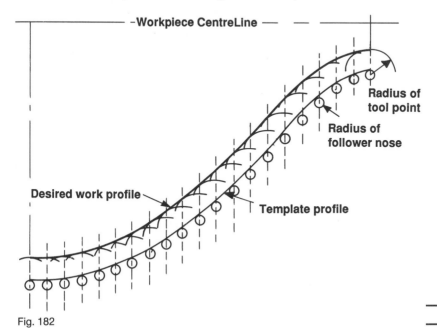

Fig. 182

(4) On the centres of these radii draw a small circle whose radius is equal to that of the template follower, or which closely approximate to the shape of the follower nose.
(5) Draw a curve touching these small circles. This is the required shape of the template, after allowing for the scale of the drawing if used.

Templates may be made from almost any material but if soft plastic (e.g. Perspex) is used care must be taken not to exert too much pressure on the tool-slide lever, as this could cause indentations in the profile.

# INDEX